Memoirs

Seize the Day

Other Books by Gideon Goosen

The Theology of Work,
(Wisconsin: Clergy Book Service, 1974).

Studying the Gospels,
(with Margaret Tomlinson) Sydney: E.J. Dwyer 1994 ; Chinese version, (Taipei: Kuangchi Cultural Group, 2007).

Religion in Australian Culture: an Anthropological View.
(Strathfield: St Pauls Publications, 1997).

Australian Theologies: Themes and methodologies into the third millennium,
(Strathfield: St Pauls Publications, 2000).

Bringing Churches Together: A Popular Introduction to Ecumenism,
(Sydney: E.J.Dwyer, 1993, & Geneva: WCC, 2001) and *Introduzione all'ecumenismo* (Torino: Claudiana, 2007).

Spacetime and Theology in Dialogue,
(Wisconsin: Marquette University Press, 2008).

Hyphenated Christians: Towards a Better Understanding of Dual Religious Belonging,
(Berne: Peter Lang, 2011).

Saving Catholics: A Workbook for Reform and Renewal in the Catholic Church,
(Reservoir, Victoria: Morning Star Publishing, 2018).

Clericalism: Stories from the Pews,
(Melbourne: Coventry Press, 2020).

After a lifetime of teaching, Gideon Goosen has the common touch: the ability to put big ideas in easily understandable language. Leavened with humour and anecdote, he tells the story of his journey to ecumenism, from his early years in Apartheid South Africa to the post-Vatican II Catholic Church.

He has learned to overcome dualism in many forms: Afrikaans/English, Catholic/Calvinist, black/white, clerical/lay, body/soul. This maturing thought, born of experience, informs his plain and honest reflections on topics such as church reform, clericalism, sexuality and death. A book many Catholics will cherish and enjoy.

John D'Arcy May
Irish School of Ecumenics
Trinity College, Dublin

Gideon takes time to reflect on his memories, navigating across continents, regional wars, a world war, while confronting racial tensions, prejudices and religious differences. Gideon has written his story for his family.

This is a book that celebrates successes and helps make sense of confusion, as Gideon opens his arms to creation in all its forms whilst in each moment raising his heart to his God.

Liz O'Callaghan
Former School Principal,
Diocese of Parramatta

Gideon Goosen has shared his life journey, relationships, travels and his responses to the radical change that has marked recent Catholic Christianity. Many of my generation will find themselves in this story. A younger generation may come to understand where we have come from in such a short period of time.

Francis J. Moloney, SDB, AM, FAHA
Catholic Theological College
Adjunct Senior Lecturer in Church History
University of Divinity

Memoirs

Seize the Day

Gideon Goosen

COVENTRY PRESS

Published in Australia by
Coventry Press
33 Scoresby Road
Bayswater VIC 3153

ISBN 9781922589491

Copyright © Gideon Goosen 2024

All rights reserved. Other than for the purposes and subject to the conditions prescribed under the *Copyright Act*, no part of this publication may be reproduced, stored in a retrieval system, or transmitted in any form or by any means, electronic, mechanical, photocopying, recording or otherwise, without the prior permission of the publisher.

Scripture quotations are from the *Jerusalem Bible* copyright © 1966 by Darton Longman & Todd Ltd and Doubleday and Company Ltd.

Catalogue-in-Publication entry is available from the National Library of Australia: http://catalogue.nla.gov.au

Cover design by Ian James – www.jgd.com.au
Text design by Coventry Press
Set in Tex Gyre Pagella
Printed in Australia

DEDICATION

To my dear wife, Caroline, our wonderful children - Naomi, Rebecca, Jonathan - and our delightful grandchildren - Saskia, Ziggy, Freya, Poppy, Zadie, Olive and Rosie.

Contents

Introduction	9
1. Things to live and die for	13
2. The rise of a youngster	30
3. How to be Catholic	50
4. Holy Mother and Unholy Father	70
5. The trick of matric	80
6. By the skin of my teeth	96
7. Travelling this beautiful planet	106
8. Walking together	127
9. Life without end	140
Endnotes	164

Introduction

In my lifetime, I have been privileged in a myriad of ways. One way is that neither I nor my siblings,[1] have ever had to cope directly with a war in our homeland.

I have been aware of many conflicts. I was born during WWII (Second World War) and four years old when the war ended. I had three uncles in the defence forces, one each in the army, navy and air force, and, thankfully, none of them lost their life during WWII.

Then followed a series of seemingly never-ending conflicts during my lifetime. They were: Israel-Palestine (1944-), Korea (1950-1953), Vietnam (1955-1975), Bosnia (1992-1995), Kosovo (1998-1999), Afghanistan (2001-2021), Falklands (1982), Syria (2011-), Gulf (1990-1991), Iraq (2013-2017), Yemen (2014-), ISIS (2014-), and Ukraine (2022-).

There are other conflicts and emergencies that one could add to this depressingly woeful list like the Irish troubles (1992-1998), but you get the point that humankind on this planet always seems to be fighting somewhere, sometime, somehow.

The world has certainly changed over the years. So have I. I can also recall how, in the 1950s, I heard or read somewhere that 'China is like a sleeping giant. Someday it will wake up'. Little did I realise I would see that day. I also used to wonder what life was like in the 'Far East', without knowing I would end up living in the Far East (Australia)!

I can also recall when I was about the age of nine or ten, reading the newspapers with my older brother to find out how the Americans were doing in the Korean War. Any progress they made was applauded. In reality, I had no idea of how true it was to say that, in war, there are no winners. It certainly made no impact on my daily life.

In one lifetime, you have to be aware of these issues if you wish to make a contribution, however small, to curbing these destructive tendencies, to making the world a better place in which to live. Of course not everyone is focused on making a positive contribution in life. I am thinking of that enigma of *homo sapiens* who appears likeable and convincing but is evil within, like the infamous Blue Mountains murderer, Frank Butler.[2]

The more common alternative to making a positive contribution, is – simply and blissfully – to glide or blunder through life without giving any thought as to what kind of world we are leaving to the next generation. It is not good enough to sit in a corner and simply consume oxygen! The unexamined life is not worth living as Socrates used to say!

So why is it worth writing down one's own life history, one's memories? A well-known anti-Apartheid activist, the Dominican priest, Albert Nolan, could not see any point in it. Is it to amuse? To instruct? Or pass on wisdom to the next generation? Or simply to satisfy someone's curiosity?

Well, all of these. It is always wise to learn from someone else that life is, in part, about learning from others and avoiding the mistakes of the past while we fashion the future. If we can be amused, if we can be inspired along the way, all the better.

So sharing one's story is not a bad reason to write a memoir. What follows is a memoir, a recollection of some events in my life, rather than an autobiography which is more like telling the complete story of a life 'from the

Introduction

womb to the tomb' or, alternatively and, more basically, 'from the sperm to the worm'. I do not agree that memoirs, or autobiographies for that matter, should be written for the sake of self-aggrandisement, justifying one's career, apologising for one's mistakes in life, for settling old scores or trying to ensure the longevity of one's legacy. One should leave that to more objective and critical observers.

We live in a world today with huge – some would say, potentially catastrophic – problems. Many of these have accumulated since the industrial revolution. I am referring to such issues as the decline of natural resources, population growth, food insecurity, poverty, threat of nuclear weapons, epidemics, new uncontrolled technologies and climate change in all its dimensions such as air, water and land pollution. There are other factors no doubt that flow from these.

One of the most striking changes over the last century is that we are moving from a pretty myopic view of ourselves and our life, to beginning to see the bigger picture – the planet Earth in the context of the whole of universe as something that has evolved over 13.8 billion years. We are beginning to realise in a new way that we are earthlings, we belong to the earth, one of many planets. In terms of when we have evolved, we are johnnies-come-lately, arriving at a minute to midnight.

We are beginning to feel connected to all of life, be it animals, flora and fauna, insects or rocks. This is quite a revolutionary conversion although it might be re-claiming a view we once had thousands of years ago. Climate change is one of the catalysts of this change in outlook.

In his Gospel, John talks about Jesus as coming so that we may have life to the full. I like this phrase. It suggests giving life a red hot go! It suggests 'seizing the day' as Flacco said in his *Fifth Oration*. I feel that my life has been a happy and full one, and in turn I wish the same for others, hence the title of this memoir.

1
Things to live and die for

One of the striking incidents relating to values in life, I often think of, is that of the Czech student, Jan Palach. When Caroline and I visited Prague in 2001, our hotel was near the picturesque Old Town Square where one could sit in the sun and share a *Pilsner Urquell* with friends. On one of our daily excursions we strolled to the Wenceslas Square where there is a commemorative plaque to the student Jan Palach. He was the twenty-year-old student who self-immolated in 1968 in one of the many protest suicides against the soviets who put an end to the Prague Spring under Dubcek. The memorial is at ground level in front of the National Museum, and near the Statue of Wenceslas I, Duke of Bohemia.

This heroic incident demonstrates how utterly committed some people are to their values. In this case, the value was the freedom of the Czech people and their human rights. I can only admire people who are so committed to their values that they are prepared to die for them. Jan Palach was not the only one to self-immolate at that time. There are many such examples in history and in current times if we think of WWII, Taiwan, Ukraine, Tibet and Poland.

Values we live for

Values have played a big role in my life as we shall see. The example of Jan Palach continues to inspire me. I have had a privileged life. It has been my fortune to have lived in three different continents – Africa, Europe and Australia – and to have travelled to many exciting cities, like New Orleans, New York, Santiago, Quito, Istanbul, Rome, Venice, Paris, Berlin, Graz, Geneva, Jerusalem, Singapore, and travelled around countries like the USA, the British Isles, and other European countries.

In South America, Caroline and I had the privilege of seeing heritage sites of world fame, like the Galapagos Islands, Manchu Picchu and Cusco (the capital of the Inca Empire in the 13th century) with its stone wall complex known as Sacsayhuamán (pronounced as 'sexywoman' by the guide which drew the anticipated mirthful response from our group); and in Europe, breathtaking sites like New Grange, Stonehenge, the Eiffel Tower, *Deutsches Eck* where the Mosel joins the Rhine, the Monument to the Battle of the Nations (1813) at Leipzig when Napoleon was defeated, St Peter's Basilica in Rome, *Hagia Sophia* in Istanbul and The Dome of the Rock, Jerusalem, which is one the oldest extant works of Islamic architecture.

There is an old Chinese saying that says: 'a journey of thousand miles begins with a single step'. I am not promising a thousand miles, you will be relieved to know, but this is the first step in recording some memories and values from the past. The above places I visited concern our common human heritage. This heritage seems to me to run the risk of being overlooked in contemporary western society with its emphasis on unfettered development, GNP growth, utilitarianism and consumerism. We need to be more critical of our modern society and its values.

In this regard, I think of the way some indigenous people in the early seventeenth century viewed European people and how they lived. The following critical excerpt highlights flaws in the European value system both then and now. The citation from the writings of a French missionary, Father Pierre Biard, working with the Mi'kmaq in Nova Scotia, is a blistering attack on the European way of life. He writes that the Mi'kmaq say:

> '... *you are always fighting and quarrelling among yourselves; we live peaceably. You are envious and are all the time slandering each other; you are thieves and deceivers; you are covetous, and are neither generous nor kind; as for us, if we have a morsel of bread we share it with our neighbour*'.[3]

This insight is well worth considering when one looks back on the way one was brought up and the values that were inculcated. Such a criticism is always at the back of my mind as I think over the various influences on my life.

My mother was full of praise for the inspiring book *A Fortunate Life* by the Australian author, Albert 'Bert' Facey, published in 1981. I read it on her recommendation some years ago. It was an impressive and inspiring read. The overwhelming thought for me was how could a person who faced such tough times in his life end up so grateful for what he did have. In many ways, I also feel very grateful for all the love, good times and opportunities I have had.

When today you look around at the global situation, you note that there are 800 million who go to bed hungry every night, millions who have few opportunities to get a good education and for whom job opportunities are scarce, and 82.4 million displaced people.[4] The quality of life across the global board appears very uneven.

I recall, in the summer of 1969, the German man (and his wife) with whom I boarded for a few weeks in Bonn, ('West Germany' in those days). I was at the Friederich Wilhelm University of Bonn at the time learning basic German. Every mealtime, this elderly man would tell me stories about the wars. Unfortunately for him, his date of birth made him old enough to be in WW1 and young enough to be WWII.

His stories always started off with the phrase 'Im ersten Weltkrieg...' or, 'Im zweiten Weltkrieg...' So although I knew which war he was talking about, because of my lack of German, I could not follow the details of his descriptions. What struck me was that this man's whole life was soaked in his vivid memories of the two world wars. How unlucky is that! I am very fortunate and lucky not to have fought in any world wars. Although I was born during WWII, I never suffered directly from it.

Another book well worth reading for its many gems, is *Eddie Jaku, The Happiest Man on Earth*, by an Auschwitz survivor, Eddie Jaku. He recalls how his father told him, 'If you are lucky enough to have money and a nice house, you can afford to help those who don't. This is what life is all about. To share your good fortune'. He also added that 'the important things in life – friends, family, kindness – are far more precious than money. A man is worth more than his bank account'.[5]

This latter sentiment is borne out by the research of the authors of *The Dawn of Everything*, where they point out how some people preferred to live in Native American Communities rather than European ones, because of the qualities of 'mutual care, love and above all happiness' they encountered there.[6]

Eddie Jaku also points out the futility of jealousy in life. There is no point in making oneself sick in trying to keep up with the Joneses. The advice is to be happy with what one has and not look over the fence to see what others have got.[7] Happiness also gets his attention. 'Happiness comes from inside yourself and from the people you love. And if you are healthy and happy, you are a millionaire.'[8] His positive outlook on life is reflected in his beautiful blessing:

May you always have lots of love to share,
Lots of good health to spare,
And lots of good friends who care.[9]

Eddie Jaku had also thought about work and what it means. This was of interest to me as, at one period, I focused on the meaning of work during my studies. As so many millions of us work from morning to evening every day, what do we think of work? Is it pointless? Is it only a means of getting money to pay for your bills? I was curious to know what others thought of it.

Eddie was very practical on this issue. He said work was our contribution to a free and safe life for all. Eddie was a toolmaker, so to go to a hospital and see them using instruments that he made gave him great happiness. Teachers enrich the lives of young people and a chef brings great pleasure into our world by his dishes.[10]

But he did not consider all the monotonous and repetitive jobs like sticking labels on tin cans in a factory, or keying in data on a computer or indeed, jobs of a maintenance nature. However it is important to try to see the positive contribution that one's work makes to society.

A garbage collector is doing a very valuable service by clearing away our garbage. I have never reflected much on this because, growing up, our garbage was always collected, so we took it for granted. But later in life, while living in Rome, I experienced days when the garbage, because of a strike, was not collected and remained on the kerbside in summer in the stinking heat emitting putrid smells. This brought home to me in a very direct way the value of the service I had previously taken for granted. It is obvious that most people would not choose tedious tasks like cleaning toilets, garbage collecting, cleaning trains, or repetitive factory work if they could do something more inspiring and creative. In my experience, everyone likes to feel others appreciate their work.

I was pleasantly surprised when, in the 1980s, I initiated an annual review of my colleagues' teaching work when they were given a chance to speak about their work. This was not a formal review to go on their record or to be used for promotions. This was an off-the-record chat about their work. What an eye-opener it proved to be for me!

As these sessions took much longer than I anticipated, I realised that people simply wanted to talk about their work as this demonstrated that someone else was interested in what they did. Their work had value in someone else's eyes. I wonder how many workers today are given the chance to chat to their bosses or supervisors about their work? This informal chat also surely adds to the productivity of the worker who now feels more positive about their contribution to the workplace.

I was born into a home which had love, dedication and respect at its heart. I enjoyed a good education first at a convent school, then at a Christian Brothers School. I then joined the Christian Brothers and, given the chance to get a teacher's certificate, teach in schools, and then do various courses at university which led to job opportunities such as teaching theology at tertiary level. I became a theologian by profession.[11]

This is not an easy profession to explain to others. Socially, it can be difficult to introduce yourself. Often when people say, 'and what do you do for a profession?' I respond, 'I teach theology'. The follow-up comment is, 'you teach *geology*?' To which I reply, 'no, *theology*; actually, the two are not that dissimilar. In *geology* you study the age of the rocks, and in theology you study the *Rock of Ages*'.

I have my friend Graham English, artist and colleague, to thank for this witty observation. (Today, I might say I was like Thomas Berry, a 'geologian', that is, someone who tries to reconnect humanity with God's great work, the Earth.)[12] Given today's ignorance of theology, I sometimes take the easy way out and say I teach 'philosophy' because most people have some idea of that subject.

Teaching theology at tertiary level has its pros and cons. Allow me to generalise. The undergraduate students are interested in getting their degree, in doing what is necessary to pass a unit or subject. Their interest is not necessarily in the content of the unit. Thus sometimes the students show a disheartening lack of understanding the issues but are most anxious that they know what content will be examined.

The postgraduate students, on the other hand, are interested in the topic and the theories associated with it. They have a certain life experience that the undergraduates do not have. This enables them to question theories and statements in class and provoke engaging discussion. If teaching methodology is discussed, the postgraduate might well have a number of years of classroom teaching behind them and possibly a family of two or three children they have brought up. Their experience is practical as well as theoretical.

Another point is this: postgraduate students tend to withdraw altogether from a unit if their other-life commitments do not allow it. Thus one is left with a class in which everyone is committed. Those who could not give their all have withdrawn. This means that the overall passing rate will be high. This is different to the undergraduates where quite a few can attend poorly, seldom engage, hope to pass, but end up failing. Consequently, the class pass rate will suffer.

Some would see teaching religion as dull and boring. However, much depends on the methods used as well as the topics. If teaching religion is just indoctrination, one can appreciate that it would turn some people off. If, however, it aims to get students to think critically as well as be informed, it can be an exciting and rewarding experience.

I found there are many topics that impinge on their lives. Let me list some: understanding world religions (highly topical if your Christian son or daughter is about to marry a Muslim); the attitudes of some Christians to homosexuals; the understanding of marriage and sexuality in a society where the divorce rate is about 33%; the problem of assisted dying; the meaning of justice in a world where social or 'structural' sin is everywhere; the degradation of the Earth (and pollution) seen as an injustice to the next generation; the practice of racism among Christians and others. The topics go on.

The fact of Australia being such a multicultural society is an important factor in learning. There can be much cross-fertilisation of ideas in a class of many cultures. I recall a discussion we had in a postgraduate class on the social teachings of the Catholic Church and the Henderson poverty line. At a certain point, a student from Sri Lanka who had been patiently listening to the enthusiastic discussion, spoke up and said, 'in Australia, you have no idea of poverty'.

Likewise, with the rise of feminism, women participants while theologising, could raise all kinds of issues that had been overlooked in Christianity. Such issues include the misogynist attitudes of some Christian leaders towards women, the issue of the sexual abuse of minors by ordained men, and also the dark, largely unexplored territory of the sexual abuse and domestic violence perpetrated on the wives of clergymen.

What I found most rewarding teaching undergraduates was an introductory unit on the New Testament where students were helped to move from a fundamentalist understanding of the Bible to a more enlightened one involving modern scholarship. Students initially saw their faith as threatened but, with time, began to appreciate the fruits of scholarship. This was done on occasions with parental feedback saying the lecturers were wrong and heretical! Catholic parents of a certain age never had the opportunity of studying the Bible in an enlightened way. Education of the laity at parish level in Bible studies was close to zero.

I must register my thanks to the Christian Brothers for the time I spent with them, and for the solid education and support they gave me. I also have had the opportunity to live, study and then work in Europe and travel to many parts of the world. That sounds very fortunate when you look at the world population and the great divide between the 'haves' and the 'have-nots'.

By a quirk of fate, I was born into a society that belonged to the 'have' group. This, I feel and have always felt, places some responsibility on me to do something about the great divide. I also feel I have not done enough. I have much for which I am grateful. My father and mother, the family I grew up in, and now my present family, have all had an influence on me that I cannot measure. My wife, Caroline and my children, Naomi, Rebecca and Jonathan, have had a positive influence on me and my happiness which I cannot begin to identify. Not only them but my extended family, sisters and brothers, uncles and aunts, nieces and nephews, and grandchildren who have supported me in different ways throughout my life. This is all probably more obvious to those outside the family than those in.

I think the fact is that I take them all for granted most of the time. Moments of reflection like this are, therefore, of deep significance in telling one's story.

While on the topic of my gratitude to others who have influenced me, who have help to fashion me and my story, there is the widening circle of those in my neighbourhood, my friends and acquaintances. For me too, I must say how privileged I have been to work in education with such good colleagues and students. It is impossible to gauge their contribution to my life.

More specifically, I worked for 28 years in the institution which became the Australian Catholic University (ACU). Initially, I joined the Teachers College at North Sydney, but this over some years, with colleges in Victoria and Queensland, morphed into the ACU (1994). It was a great privilege to have worked with colleagues who were so dedicated to their work and with students (in the early days) who were committed to becoming good teachers or nurses. Naturally, the institution had the kind of managerial problems that any institution has, but it was an inspiring atmosphere in which to work.

Food for thought

One of the things we did regularly in our family, without any exceptions, was say a prayer of thanksgiving before meals (and also after meals), what was known as 'saying grace'. This custom has disappeared from many homes with the decline in religious practice and the overbearing nature of the digital world. Meals are often consumed in silence in front of a television set. At the same time, in today's world, we are being compelled to think about the future of the world and the consequences of climate change which includes a threat to our food supplies. Farmers see this clearly. It is an inescapable 'existential' threat as they say.

Fifty years ago, we did not think like this. We assumed food would go on being available for everyone (though it was not). We gave thanks because we were taught that God gives us all good things and it is simply our duty to give thanks. Today, for many, old assumptions are being questioned and sometimes discarded.

Mealtime is a time when the family comes together around a table to do what is essential for life, that is, eating. Without food we die. We share food because we realise we all need to eat and are one family. We look after each other (as well as fight from time to time – as the Mi'kmaq noted!). We are also capable of thinking beyond our nuclear family and seeing the whole world as the human family.

Everyone needs to eat to live. This aspect was sometimes mentioned by my parents. Think of all those children and adults who do not have enough to eat. About 800 million in the world. It was always possible to exclude those 800 million and just think of yourself.

But today, those who reflect have worked out that if climate change creates food shortages it will have a global effect, not just a local one. The unity of humankind is being emphasised; this contrasts sharply with the selfishness of the individualism which the West has promoted since the industrial revolution. (It is not a total surprise that, in the context of an epidemic like Covid, some anti-vaxxers, in refusing vaccination, cannot see that their actions are against the common good.)

I always appreciate the reminder – through a prayer of thanksgiving before meals with the family – that all life comes from the One Creator of all life. I am forever grateful to my parents for our family life and have tried to pass on those values to my family now.

Values came into play too when my parents chose a school for their children. As regards the culture of sending your children to a Catholic school, I can say it was the done thing, it was part of the culture of being a Catholic during that era. What I remember was that when we moved from Mafeking to Boksburg (near Johannesburg, South Africa), my mother and father choose a house to buy that was near both a convent (for my two sisters) and a Christian Brothers school for us two boys (my eldest brother was already at CBC Kimberley).

My mother seems to have had no problems of enrolment at the convent, but the principal at the Boksburg CBC told her all the relevant classes were full and he could not admit my brother and me. However, my mother would not take no for an answer. She did not give up and after some discussion with the principal pointing out that they had chosen a house close to the schools and that they were good Catholics, the principal relented and enrolled us!

My mother was not an aggressive person but when her values came into play she could be firm and resolute. Thus values come to the fore when we view life holistically and identify the big, significant actions that reveal the serious underlying values.

Add humour

Having introduced the serious topic of values above by recalling the life of Jan Palach and other sources of inspiration, I want to add to my story, in a lighter vein, the element of humour.

I firmly believe humour is an important ingredient in a happy and balanced life. Without it life would be awfully dull and onerous, but with it, we can manage the worst things that life has to throw at us. I frequently recall an encouraging rhyming couplet I came across in my younger days which went:

From the day we are born,
till we ride in the hearse,
there is nothing so bad,
that it couldn't be worse.

This attitude of always trying to look on the bright side of things has helped me throughout my life. Humour is the spice of life. As the words of the song go: 'always look on the bright side of life'! What follows are some of the humourous incidents I recall from the past.

I have been in the teaching profession all my adult career. You learn a lot as you progress through any profession. Among other things, when you learn a few languages, you remain cautious of what they call 'false friends', that is, words that sound the same in both languages but whose meanings are very different. In Italian, for example, 'parente' does not mean 'parents' in English, but 'relatives'. Bearing this in mind, I can recall an incident regarding a visiting professor from Europe, at the tertiary college in Cedara, South Africa, where I taught for nearly three years. His mother tongue was French and he presumed he knew enough English to be able to teach in that language.

At the end of each lesson, when the bell indicated that the lecture time was over, he, in full flight explaining some obtuse concept, would exclaim in English, 'damage!', thinking he was saying in English the equivalent of the French '*quel dommage*!' This left the students scratching their heads in puzzlement.

Another humorous tale comes from Ireland as many do. While there, I was able to tell this joke to a research group at Maynooth. The story went like this: I took a bus trip one Saturday down to Glendalough and on the way stopped at a Rathdrum which had a corner shop that looked like it might sell newspapers. I went inside and asked the kindly lady if they sold the newspaper. She said, 'Yes, we do'. Then she asked a rather unusual question: 'Would you like today's or yesterday's?' Without hesitation, and mildly irritated by the question, I said, 'Today's please'. 'Well', she replied, 'could you come back tomorrow!'

While I think of it, here is another story from Ireland. I think of the motorist who was lost somewhere on the west coast, stopping a local farmer and asking: 'Could you please tell me how to get to Dublin from here? The farmer gave the matter some deep and serious thought and then advised the motorist: 'If I were going to Dublin I would not be going from here!' Amusing as this story may sound, funny things do happen in Ireland. I can remember travelling by car with Caroline and my brother-in-law from Dublin going south towards Tipperary. We noticed that a certain road sign said 'Fethard 25 miles' and then after a further twenty minutes of travelling in the car, the next road sign said 'Fethard 35 miles'. I had heard about changing the road signs in war in order to confuse the enemy but not in peace time!

Another humorous event occurred in Switzerland some years later. Caroline and I were spending a few relaxing days at a hotel in Villeneuve, a small, attractive village in the canton of Vaud, on the shores of Lake Geneva not far from the town of Aigle. It was a small, modest hotel but in a beautiful setting near the lake. As we had been travelling for a few days, we had clothes that needed to be washed. My bundle of clothes included a pair of socks that my younger daughter had given me for my birthday. They were modern (or 'cool') socks in the sense that one was blue and the other orange! So we handed in our washing knowing it would take at least a day.

The next day, we went down to the reception to enquire about our washing. The owner and his wife were full of apologies and visibly worried. The Swiss take life seriously and are not normally given to a spontaneous or frivolous outburst of laughter. The owner began to explain to us in a serious voice that they had lost two of our socks and only had one blue and one orange one left. He had conscientiously been to the shops and purchased a new pair to replace those he had so carelessly lost.

Caroline, my polyglot wife, who speaks fluent French, smiled and explained to them that those two socks were in fact a pair, one blue, one orange, and that they had lost nothing. Well, to see the Swiss couple break out in laughter when they realised the odd socks were in fact a pair was something to behold!

Now let me go back in time to Germany and an earlier event while I was a student. It was in Munich, the month of October, about 1969, and the famous Oktoberfest. For those not familiar with this festival, it is basically a fortnight-long, beer-drinking and funfair annual festival in Bavaria from late September to early October. The festival was held, not in the well-known pub, *Hofbräuhaus* in Munich, but in the *Thereseinplatz*, which is a large open-air space.

I was there with student friends of mine and, as I recall, we only made it on the last evening of the festival. I need to add that I already had a beard in those days. As we arrived rather late, the drinking was well under way and the mood was distinctly jolly. I recall the images of busty German women carrying incredible numbers of beer steins to crowed tables amid roars of approval and gratitude. As we strolled around looking for a free table, three very jovial young women came towards us and one came up to me and kissed me giggling and saying (in German) 'a kiss without a beard is like soup without salt'! And then she and her friends floated away and disappeared into the night.

Another humorous trick of a very different kind was this. I liked to play the trick on young tertiary students related to their ignorance of the Bible. It was noticeable how in the 1990s and onwards, young adults (especially

Catholics) came through their schooling years without much knowledge of religion (both Christianity and other faiths) and of the Bible. I used to ask them if they had heard of *Gideon's Bible*, which used to be left in hotel rooms for clients to read if they had nothing else. Some students had heard of that Bible. 'Well', I would add, 'I wrote that Bible!' 'Did you really, sir? Gosh!', came the amazed response.

This brings to mind another trick I tried in Ireland. It was 1973, at the time of a fuel crisis in Europe. Caroline and I happened to be travelling by car in Ireland at the time. Actually we were visiting her parents who lived in Myrtleville not far from Cork. The problem was how to get a full tank of petrol.

As I remember it, one was only allowed a certain small amount at the bowser. In order to get even a little you had to queue up in your car. We had heard the case of one innovative Irishman who dressed up in a long white coat and then went to the end of the queue and said to the drivers in turn, 'If you want to speed things up, you can pay me now so that when we reach the bowser it will be quicker'. He accepted their money and, when he had enough, he jumped on his bicycle and took off!

My approach was somewhat less courageous but took into account that I was in Catholic Ireland. I said to the attendant at the bowser: 'If you give me a full tank I will send you a papal blessing when I get back to Rome!' – knowing that you could buy a blessing at *Standa* (a supermarket like *Woolworths* or *Sainsbury's*). Needless to say, my offer was not accepted.

Having discussed the importance of values in life, starting with Jan Palach, and then moved on to the importance of adding some humour to our lives, it is time to move forward with the early days of my story.

2
The rise of a youngster

I was born in South Africa. I am inclined to say 'born free and superior', because at that time the apartheid regime was based on the assumption that the whites were privileged over the indigenous people of colour.

I remember a few incidents that formed my initial childhood feelings and thoughts about racial prejudice, although at that time (I was about 10 years old), I did not know the words 'racial prejudice' or 'racism'. These experiences branded an indelible impression on my consciousness that has stayed with me down the years.

The words we use for the indigenous people world-wide, has changed over the decades reflecting a slow change in understanding the issues and a slower change in attitudes. In South Africa in the 1950s, the term for black people was 'natives'.

Actually, the whole of society was divided into four groups: Europeans, Natives, Coloureds and Indians. This could be simplified further into two groups: Society consisted of 'Europeans' and 'non-Europeans' (in Afrikaans, the language of the Dutch descendants, the terms were, 'Blankes' or 'nie-Blankes') or 'Natives', 'Coloureds' or 'Indians'. I remember how many things in public life were labelled 'European' or 'non-European'. For example, a bench in a park would have this label and you needed to check that the train you caught was labelled 'European' if you were white. On my parents' marriage certificate, in the top left-hand corner, an 'E' indicates the European race to which they belonged.

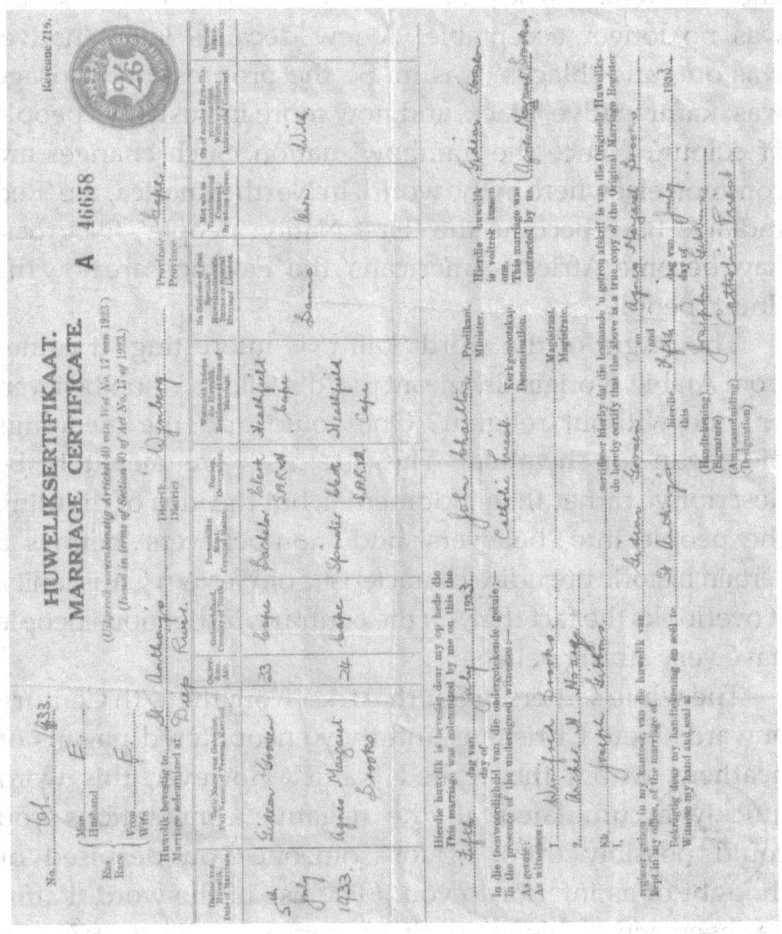

Certificate of my parents marriage.
Note racial reference top lefthand corner.

The worst possible word to use for blacks was 'kaffir'. At least one of our text books in school used 'kaffir' but later editions quickly switched to 'native' when 'kaffir' was no longer acceptable. A few decades later, 'native' was out, and 'blacks' was in. So the progression in usage was: kaffir, native, black, and now more inclusively, 'people of colour'. Hence the 'rainbow' nation. Such changes are common elsewhere in the world. In North America, the 'Red Indians' have become the 'First Nation people', 'Negroes' have become 'African-Americans', the 'Eskimos' are now the 'Inuit' people.

The origin of the word 'kaffir' is interesting. It comes from Arabic. It originally meant the 'disbeliever', 'non-believer' or 'one without religion'. One could add the meanings of 'pagan' or 'heathen'. These terms were meant to be descriptive rather than judgmental, but the idea of dividing the people into 'believers' and 'non-believers' betrays a certain historic prejudice characteristic of Western Christianity. It overlooks the fact that, on the contrary, indigenous people have very strong beliefs.

The white settlers in South Africa from the 17th Century onwards were Christians and they encountered pagans or heathens whom they called 'kaffir'. However, this word quickly accumulated all the negative connotations you could possibly think of for someone you despised or thought of as inferior to you. (The use of the word 'kaffir' has been actionable in South African courts since 1976). In colonial Australia too, the indigenous people were given derogatory names like 'bongo', 'abo', that gave way to 'Aboriginal person' or 'Aborigine' and now 'First Nation People'. Interestingly enough, the equivalent words for indigenous people in other cultures such as Malaysia, India and Sri Lanka – as far as I know – did not acquire a pejorative meaning.

In terms of my enculturation into white society in South Africa, I can vividly recall the following story. It was an incident outside a café not far from where we lived. It was always busy with black and white people coming and going, being on the corner of two quite busy roads in my hometown.

The blacks often seem to hang around outside the café talking and perhaps waiting for a friend who was in the café buying something. There was also a bus stop outside the café. If I was going into the café I would need to thread between and around those standing outside.

On this particular day a white man walked directly into a black man who was in his way instead of swinging to avoid him. This evoked a grunt from the black man. The white man took this as meaning an objection and so spoke roughly to him and soon a fisticuffs broke out. Someone must have called the police who came with their paddy wagon. The police took no time in shoving the black man unceremoniously into the paddy wagon without any attempt to find out what had happened. This is how it seemed to me.

From my perspective, as a young boy of about ten years old who saw the whole episode, I knew that this was unjust as the white man had provoked the incident in an aggressive manner. It also taught me where the police stood in these matters. The blacks were always in the wrong.

I also recall how a small group of us youngsters used to go into Johannesburg by train on a Saturday morning to purchase small items at the Scout shop. It was my older brother, his friend who was even older, myself and another friend. Walking on the sidewalk in the city, I noticed how this older friend of my brother would pretend to allow blacks walking in the opposite direction to proceed by moving his shoulder backwards pretending to make room for them to pass, but, at the last moment, he would bring his shoulder around and into play and so knock the oncoming blacks with his shoulder. The blacks knew they couldn't retaliate because to do so would involve the police and they would be found to be in the wrong. He would do this repeatedly with a wink of his eye which said to me: 'watch this'. Intuitively, I knew this was provocative and malicious.

Overall, growing up in Apartheid South Africa, one quickly saw that the whites were prejudiced against the blacks and the police were on the side of the whites. It would take another forty years, to 1994, before all the blacks in the country had the vote.

Part of the success of *apartheid* in those years was the strategic way the government had separated the blacks from the whites. Segregation was everywhere: schools, transport, churches, you name it. Whites were not allowed into black neighbourhoods, or 'locations' (townships) as they called them unless they had a permit.

This kept whites ignorant of the terrible living conditions of the blacks. Out of sight, out of mind. Most of them had no running water and no electricity. They had to scrape together some firewood for heating or cooking. (At the same time, in our neighbourhood, bags of coal were sold to the whites off the back of a truck operated by blacks.)

Although I noticed some things were patently unjust towards the blacks, there were other things I did not identify as unjust. For example, the lack of educational resources, or medical resources for the blacks. These issues were hidden from us growing up. Thinking about this later in life, my conclusion is that growing up in the apartheid era was like being in a smoke-filled room – one notices the smoke less and less with the passage of time. It is only when one goes out of the room that one realises how unhealthy it was!

Although I could see some injustices, I had interiorised many negative attitudes towards blacks as I grew up in South Africa. It was not until I went to Europe to study in 1967 that I began to see things politically in a different and more objective light.

I like the image of the smoke-filled room. Colonisers from western countries grew up in an atmosphere where, according to the popular prejudices of the times, the white Christians were called upon to enlighten and civilise the rest of the world. They had superior knowledge, religion and morality. The rest of the world were savages. These prejudices have been clearly exposed as further historical research into those colonial days becomes available.

But to return to my story. Migrating to Australia in 1976, it was a relief to notice that people, by and large, were treated equally be they whatever colour, culture or religion. On one particular car outing shortly after arriving in Australia, we were surprised to see a sign on the side of the road which read: *Natives for Sale*. We had thought slavery was no longer practised in Australia!

The generosity of most Australians towards migrants is a distinguishing characteristic. Again the Christian Brothers assisted me and my family in settling in Australia and indeed my first job was teaching at Aquinas College, Ringwood, Melbourne.

From a cultural viewpoint, you can say that you absorb the culture into which you are born. That is the process of enculturation. It happens only once in your life. As you grow up, you are enculturated into the culture around you. Thereafter only changes, or adjustments, (called 'acculturation') can be made to your culture. So if you go and live in Europe, as I did, my culture slowly modified in many ways.

In Australia, it is interesting to observe the process of acculturation whereby elements (customs, attitudes, theories, philosophies) taken from American society have become part of Australian culture. I am thinking of customs associated with, for example, Halloween, Black Friday Sales, basketball, high-fives, but also more profound aspects of life, like individualism, consumerism, love of wealth, disrespect for democracy and truth, and extremism.

Furthermore, we are seeing how hardened negative attitudes to Muslims, for example, are slowly changing as people discover that Muslims are normal people who live, love, cry, wish the best for their children and enjoy life, as they do. Attitudes towards Aborigines have improved over the last 200 years, but, as the 2023 Referendum vote indicated, there are still many uninformed negative attitudes.

Change comes slowly. Will it happen in other global instances cases as well? I am thinking of the cultural attitudes of Chinese towards the Muslim Uighurs in China's Xinjiang Provence. Will that change with time?

A big change occurred in South Africa towards the end of the twentieth century. F. W. de Klerk died in 2021 at the age of 85. He was president in South Africa 1989-1994 and took the initiative to release Nelson Mandela from prison in 1991 and move toward a new democratic multiracial ('rainbow nation') country.

He is interesting in that he read the signs of the times, realising that South Africa was suffering economically because of the sanctions applied by various countries due to its unjust apartheid system. He apologised in 1993 for the first time, regretting the loss of freedom and dignity inflicted upon blacks under apartheid.

From 1948 to 1993 is 45 years – a long time to work out the injustice of the apartheid system, although in other parts of the world grave injustices also take a long time to resolve. I am thinking of the dispossession of land and human rights that the Palestinians have suffered since 1947. But that is only one example.

As most of us act from a variety of motivations, I suppose F. W. de Klerk was also motivated by more than one reason. The main reasons I would think were the injustice of the apartheid system as well as the penalty South Africa was paying due to the economic sanctions. Nonetheless, he and Nelson Mandela were together awarded the 1993 Nobel Peace Prize.

Mandela's example of forgiveness and reconciliation is quite stunning. After 27 years in jail, he could still forgive and move forward! This example is truly exceptional given how many other leaders, religious or secular, are not able to forgive. In the 2013 movie made of him, entitled *Long Walk to Freedom*, I recall how after his installation as president, his white and black bodyguards were jostling for power. They appealed to Mandela. His wise response was, 'Now that we have a multi-coloured republic, you will just have to learn to work together'. He was a truly great statesman, rather than just another politician.

History will have to be corrected as, in the west, most of the textbooks were written by the conquerors, the whites, and gave the history from the perspective of the colonialists. This happens in all colonised countries. Australia is no exception. Only now are the First Nation people insisting on highlighting the Australian Wars when over 400 Aboriginal people were massacred as opposed to a dozen whites. David Marr has done a convincing job in exposing the crimes committed against Aborigines in Queensland in the 19th Century.[13] The truth-telling is finally being embraced.

In South Africa, the story of how King Dingane betrayed the white *voortrekkers* and slaughtered them is emphasised at the expense of all the injustices inflicted on the indigenous occupants since the Dutch invaded the country under Van Riebeeck at the end of the 17th century. That emphasis must also be put in context.

Parents

I have always believed that parents play a critical role in most people's lives. They are part of the environment one inhales. My father was born into a large family in a small, winegrowing, Afrikaans-speaking town, not far from Cape Town, in the Western Cape, called Tulbagh. It was named after the Dutch Colonial Governor at the time, Ryk Tulbagh. Today, the graceful Dutch-styled gabled houses are still seen in Tulbagh. However, the area was originally occupied by the First Nation peoples, called the Khoi and Bushmen.

My father's side of the family were of Dutch Calvinist background although his mother was a descendent of the first large scale migration of the French Huguenots who arrived in South Africa in 1687. French surnames were subsequently changed into adjusted local ways of pronouncing them. *Villion* became *Viljoen* for example, and *Le Clerq* became *De Klerk*. Others French names appeared as Cillers, Delport, De Villiers, De Plessis, du Toit, Labuschagne (from la Buscagne). The French Huguenots also influenced the language. So, for example, Afrikaans has a double negative which comes from the French '*ne... pas*'.

That the Huguenots came to Tulbagh all that time ago, is interesting and significant. Here, a little history helps. The Huguenots were a religious group of Protestants who followed the teaching of the French Reformer, John Calvin, and were persecuted by the French Catholic government. The Calvinists had the custom of using Old Testament names for their children, so not surprisingly, I was named *Gideon* which occurs in Chapter 6 of the biblical book called *Judges*. The name is not familiar to Anglo-Saxons (unless Presbyterians). Hence for the rest of my life, when I was introduced to a new group of people (such as golfers before a round of golf), they invariably thought the name was 'Gillian'.

Of course, the name is known to the older generation, through the habit, mentioned above, of a certain corporation leaving Gideon's Bible in hotel rooms for the guests to read. (The modern equivalent is removing the Bible and making porn available on your screen.)

But I digress. During the entire period between the early part of the sixteenth century to 1787, thousands of Huguenots left their homes in France for other countries because of recurring waves of persecution. The *Edict of Nantes* (1598) had protected their religious rights but this was revoked under Louis XIV with the *Edict of Fontainebleau* in 1685. This ended legal recognition of Protestantism in France and the Huguenots were forced to either convert to Catholicism or flee as refugees. They fled, creating

Huguenot settlements all over Europe, in the United States and the Cape of Good Hope.

My father was of Protestant background before becoming a Catholic. He was very interested in the reconciliation of Calvinists and Catholics and this area of interest – known now as 'ecumenism – became my own great interest from an academic and practical viewpoint. Only after the fact did I begin to reflect and see the hidden threads of ecumenism in my family tree. My younger sister could see this and pointed it out to me.

My father worked for the South African Railways all his life and, after some transfers and promotions, ended up at the Railway HQ in Johannesburg. He came from a large family and, I presume, for economic reasons, went out to work before he had completed his high school. This was great pity as he would have enjoyed university work if he had been given a chance. His great hobby was writing for a magazine called *Die Brug*, which was a 'bridge' between Catholics and Afrikaans-speaking Calvinists.

It is interesting that more than once, people I have met have been curious to know what my background is. Is it English or Afrikaans (Boer). They usually have heard about the Boer War in 1899-1902 in South Africa. They pronounce 'Boer' like the English word 'bore' which is incorrect. Thus they ask me: Are you a 'bore'? To which I reply: well, I try not to be!

My father was bilingual in his work and at home English was our language. My mother knew some Afrikaans – enough to get by. If your education was primarily through English, you had to learn Afrikaans as a second language. I did this without great success. However when I did my B.A,

The rise of a youngster

at university I took on Afrikaans-Nederlands as a subject and was thereby forced to improve my skills.

In addition to this, I was asked to teach Afrikaans to students doing their final two years at a high school, which was demanding. Inspectors from the Education Department used to inspect me from time to time to see if our school was up to standard. Looking back, I did not seem to be fazed by these inspections. Perhaps I was conscious that teachers of Afrikaans background had to teach English in their school, and I knew that many spoke English poorly.

One incident sticks with me. I attended BA evening classes in 1959-1960 at the University in Bloemfontein while studying daytime for a teacher's certificate at the Teachers College. One of my BA subjects was English and we had an ex-Oxford professor as our lecturer for poetry. Bloemfontein being a mainly Afrikaans city, most of my fellow students in the English class were Afrikaans-speaking and their English was shaky, to say the least. Our professor had the habit of starting his lectures with colourful stories and outrageous incidents from his time in Oxford. Then he would suddenly switch and discuss a poem with us. Some students had no idea of what he was doing and would come to me afterwards to find out what was entertaining but irrelevant story-telling, and what was exam material.

I personally had no problems with those who spoke Afrikaans. There was within the Afrikaner population many who were very anti-English (and anti-Catholic), that is, against the language and against those who spoke English. This goes back to the history of South Africa when the Boers fled from the Cape to get away from British rule (the 'Great Trek').

But the British came after them (and the gold and diamonds!) in what is called the Boer War (1899-1902) during which the British conquered the Afrikaans republics in the north (The South African Republic and Orange Free State). Boers who were captured during the Boer War were put in concentration camps and treated poorly. This tragic incident branded itself indelibly into the Afrikaner psyche.

So this was the context of any contact with other schools. When I was playing rugby for our school we often played Afrikaans schools and then the hatred came to the surface. There were always some who sought a fisticuffs on the field and indeed after the game. As a youngster I noticed that the coaches/teachers never spoke to each other the way they did when we played English-speaking schools. I was annoyed that most of the teachers made no effort to promote friendship between the schools and, indeed, seem to promote ill feelings.

Later in life, as a teacher and coach, I enjoyed speaking to the teachers and coaches from Afrikaans-speaking schools. I especially appreciated the fact that many Afrikaans schools had taken up the game of cricket which was seen as a game played by English schools. (Schools were probably encouraged by the increasing number of Afrikaners who made it into the national team, which became internationally strong).

The teachers had to deal with two problems: first, they were coaching a game that was new to them, and secondly, they felt compelled to use English while playing cricket. (Later in life, I played cricket on Corfu island against the local Greeks who spoke no English with the exception of words like 'HOWZAT?' and 'OUT'.)

The rise of a youngster

The lack of knowledge of the game could be amusing. Normally, with these school cricket games, the two coaches were automatically the umpires. Umpiring cricket can be difficult. I recall on one occasion a young twelve-year old from an Afrikaans school was batting and there was an appeal for lbw from our bowler. The Afrikaans teacher gave him out but the young lad said to the teacher, 'Nie meneer, ek is nie uit nie.' ('No Sir, I am not out'). And then proceeded to tell his teacher why not. Amazingly the teacher changed his decision. I said nothing, impressed by the boldness of this young boy.

Let me now move onto my mother, Agnes. She lived a rather unusual life. She married in 1933 and my father died 31 years later. My mother then lived for a further 37 as a widow and was able to visit her five children (three boys and two girls) in various parts of the world. She had five children, eighteen grandchildren, and a number of great grandchildren. She was from Irish-Scottish-English stock.

My maternal grandmother was born in South Africa but her mother came from Galway in Ireland. My grandmother married an Englishman from London. My mother did the usual secretarial course and worked as a typist in Cape Town. Had she had the opportunity to go to university she too would have loved it.

She was an avid reader and would go to the library to take out books regularly. Her favourite joke was to quote the notice in our local library: 'Books arranged by authors in Alphabetical Order'. Her comment was: wasn't that nice of them to come in and do that!! Her knowledge of idiomatic English was always helpful when we did our homework.

Education is all about opportunities. In the days of my parents, the completion of high school, let alone university, could not be taken for granted. In my time, a university degree was quite feasible. I was, in fact, the first in our family to get a university degree. I had never stopped to note this. It was my eldest brother who on the day the newspaper had the results, said to me: 'You are first in our family to a get a degree'. I had not thought about that.

Today, our children have all had the opportunity to go to university, and took it for granted. Refugees often remind us of that privilege when they get excited at the chance to take on tertiary studies.

My mother's side of the family were Catholics and very religious in the way that people were in the 18th and 19th centuries. There were the usual devotional things to do like go to Mass, go to confession every week, eat fish on Fridays, give up something for Lent, say the rosary every night, morning and night prayers, make novenas.

Sons should become altar boys. Girls could not, but they could join the 'Children of Mary'. Your children should attend a Catholic school. Clericalism was pervasive. The laity were often the first to put a pastor on a pedestal. The pastor could do nothing wrong. So we were brought up with these assumptions.

One incident I recall quite vividly about my mother must have occurred in 1948 when I was seven years old and we were living in Mafeking, Northern Cape province at the time. My younger sister was about a year old and in great discomfort because her bowel was twisted. Every time she needed to have a bowel movement she would be crying in agony.

My mother finally had to take her for an operation to the hospital in Kimberley, some hundreds of miles away by train. My mother probably had to stay over in Kimberley a few days before she could bring my sister home. The part I remember so clearly was my mother recounting how she had to leave her baby in the hospital prior to the operation, and as she walked down the corridor to leave the hospital, she could hear her baby crying out after her.

Every mother can identify with that moment. I remembered this because, although I was six years older than my sister, I was her frequent playmate. I am glad to report that the operation was successful and normal family life could resume thereafter.

My father and mother always used to live frugally and not waste anything. They also tried to maintain their possessions in good condition. They looked after everything like clothes, furniture, plus any other possessions they had. This attitude was conveyed to us children in no uncertain terms. It has probably stuck with me ever since. Some reflection on this is called for as it links up with modern thinking about waste regarding food, clothes and possessions and the finiteness of our resources in general.

I believe part of the explanation of this frugality comes from living through the depression. Let me explain what the 'depression' was. The dates given for what is called the Great Depression are 1929-1939. It was essentially a time of economic depression sparked by the collapse of the New York stock market on 24 October 1929. For families across the world, it meant loss of jobs, high prices for food if available, and general misery with worldwide Gross Domestic Produce falling by 15%. Because it was so widespread, it was regarded as the worst economic depression of the 20th century.

After the depression, there was WWII and its aftermath. Although South Africa and Australia did not see any fighting on their soil, there was a supply problem of foods, fuel, etc., during and after the war ended.

I think this impacted on living during the depression in the 1930s. Anyone who lived through those times learnt to do with very little, because there was very little. Few clothes, little food, no money.

I was born during the war so my recollections are vague, but I can remember that butter was scarce and my mother always telling us to put only a little butter on our bread. Flour too was a problem. Perhaps supply was the issue. We were not on food vouchers but I gathered that we had to use these things sparingly without understanding why.

Strange how times change. We now live in era when people in western countries are often possessed by the spirit of acquiring things, the spirit of acquisitiveness. They feel the overpowering impulse to buy new things, be it clothes, gadgets, cars, electronic equipment or houses. Today we live in a consumer society.

I recall a graffiti instruction painted on the underbelly of a bridge on the way to Central Sydney Rail Station – a trip I took frequently. It stated boldly but accurately what society wanted me to do: *Consume, Be Silent, Die*. This was a healthy reminder for me every day on my way to work!

Today things are beginning to change. It all started with a group of people called the Club of Rome in the 1970s who pointed out that the resources of this planet were limited. This realisation coupled with climate change data and its impact on farming, air pollution and events like extreme wildfires and floods, has slowly moved people's thinking from consumerism to the need to look after this planet if we want a future on Earth.

The brakes are being slowly applied as we realise that much of our problem is our own making. The throw-away society must change direction or we will choke all life on Earth. All consumerism is a problem for us today.

The consumption mindset is not just a personal phenomenon. It refers not only to families, but industries, businesses, institutions, governments and churches. There is a tendency to want to grow without limits.

It is interesting that religions have caught the bug too. They too have tended to grow and expand, acquire new buildings, land, treasures and capital. Money is on the mind of many religious leaders like pastors and parish priests. In all the many parishes that I have lived in throughout my life, only one has had the rule that the incumbent parish priest never speaks about finances; he always leaves that to the chair of the finance committee!

Jesus and his followers never had a building called a synagogue or temple. Even after he died, his followers used houses for coming together to break bread. In general, it was only after Constantine that the organisation called 'church' started taking over Roman basilicas and turning them into churches. That was the beginning of its material expansion.

The New Testament teaches 'contentment'. A quick look at this by way of a sidetrack, will highlight the essentials of what could be a contemporary spirituality of contentment which could easily dovetail with caring for the environment.

Paul mentions contentment in his letter to the Philippians 4:10-23. He is writing to the Philippians and thanks them for expressing concern about his welfare. Paul says he has all he needs. He has known hardship, been without money and been hungry. Now he can manage with whatever he has.

There is nothing he cannot master because he has the help of God. 'I have learnt to be content with whatever I have' (Philippians 4:11).

The idea of contentment is also mentioned in 2 Corinthians 9:8 and 1 Timothy 6:6. The Greek word used in the New Testament is either 'autakes' or 'autarkeian', meaning 'sufficient or adequate in one's self, contented with one's lot'.

In 2 Corinthians 9:8, Paul says that God will send them all they need and then there will be enough left over for their good works for others. Their self-sufficiency will come from God. 1 Timothy 6:6 also mentions contentment. The author Timothy says that religion brings great rewards but only to those who are content with what they have. He adds that as long as they have food and clothes, that is, the necessities for nature and for the person, they should be content. God-sourced sufficiency is not the self-sufficiency as proposed by philosophers.

Now I am not suggesting this can be simplistically applied to today's circumstance. However, there is an urgent need to review the extent to which Christians (and other religions) have been seduced by consumerism/capitalism and the need to ask the question of what contentment could mean for us at this point in time.

We need to develop this idea of contentment, while acknowledging the legitimate claims of trade unions and others. The balance between a just wage and contentment is a delicate one to negotiate. The gap between the rich and the poor is forever widening in our modern society. The poor are deprived and paid wages too low for essential existence, while CEOs are paid obscene amounts, many times greater than the lowest wage.

Perhaps people who live on the land and First Nation people can help in forming a spirituality that includes contentment and the natural world. For people living in the outback, far from towns and shops, it is a question of necessity to make do with the essentials and not go shopping every day for new this and that. Country people find it easier to relate to others, to animals, to the natural environment. We can all learn much from them by way of weaning ourselves from the corrosive, compulsive, consumerist mentality.

To this can be added the view of time. In the west, it is linear. We move forward the whole time, and progress is always something for which we are striving. In Aboriginal culture, time can be circular. We are in time now, past, present and future. The past has gone, the future is not yet here, so all we have is the present moment. We can live in the moment and enjoy it, not worried about the past and preoccupied with the future.

Underlying all the above was the religious background for my story. What was it like growing up within Catholicism? I will follow that up now.

3

How to be Catholic

How we live as adults is influenced by the circumstances of our religious, aesthetic, moral physical, intellectual and spiritual background. The extent of the influence differs from one individual to another. I do not believe in determinism here but I definitely believe that a stronger or weaker influence is possible and can stay with us for life. I would like to investigate and describe my religious background in this chapter, hilarious as it seems in part.

Growing up with the assumptions mentioned in the previous chapter would define my early religious education. I had to go to confession every Saturday afternoon but I always struggled to think up a list of sins that were different to the previous weeks. I rarely succeeded. But I concluded that it did not make any difference as the pastor did not seem to realise I used the same list as the previous Saturday!

For those who do not know, confession is what we Catholics do when we verbally admit to our sins to a priest.

We went into a small room called the confessional. We knelt behind a curtain and spoke into the curtain to the invisible pastor. I was convinced that he could not see me until one day, after confession, he said, as I was leaving the confessional: 'Tell your dad the meeting tonight has been cancelled'. That did it for me! He knew who I was!

Then there were 'Novenas'. They are religious practices that require you to do something religious for nine occasions and then you get a spiritual reward. The one I attempted more than once went like this: you had to go to Mass every first Friday of the month for nine consecutive months (they must be consecutive!) and then you earn a free pass to heaven (technically a 'plenary indulgence'). It seemed a good deal for a young altar boy. I often had to go to serve at Mass on weekdays at the nearby Dominican convent anyway, so I reckoned I could do a novena.

The problem was with the 'nine'. I could do six or seven consecutively but then there was always a first Friday when I did not get out of bed in time. The problem was you had to go to START again, as in Monopoly, if you missed one. The rule was too tough for me. Alas, I was a novena failure!

Being an altar boy could be fun. If there was a funeral in the parish, the parish pastor would phone the school principal and ask for a few altar boys to serve. I was usually on the short list. That meant getting out of school! And we got to ride in the pastor's old dilapidated car in the back seat while holding onto the swishing holy water in a bowl.

The pastor would deliberately leave the church later than the cortege and then race across a field on a dirt road to catch up with the cortege on a main road. We enjoyed splashing the holy water around the back seats as the car hit bumps on the road. I had the feeling that the pastor secretly enjoyed the car race!

We also served at a church service called *Benediction* which usually occurred on a Sunday evening. It was called 'Rosary and Benediction'.

Let me first explain the mysterious 'thurible' which is central to this story. A thurible is a vessel like a bowl with long chains, used in Benediction. The bowl holds lighted coals or charcoal. From time to time, incense is strewn on the coals to make aromatic smoke which rises in great mysterious clouds and symbolises prayer going to heaven while making it tough for anyone who suffers from asthma. The altar boy with the incense in the thurible would kneel some metres *behind* the pastor and other servers during the service. Thus they could not see what he was up to, but the alert congregation could. The congregation would, of course, be behind the altar boy with the incense.

The normal duty of this altar boy was to gently swing the thurible from side to side, like a pendulum to keep the smoke coming. The challenge among us altar boys was: who could give the thurible a complete swing of 360 degrees during the service and not be caught out. I achieved this at least once and – I am proud to announce – was not reported.

Another aspect to this service of 'Rosary and Benediction' was walking around the interior of the church while reciting the rosary. Once a month, the 'Children of Mary' (young girls of the parish) would be dressed in their blue and white outfits and be on display. The boys liked this parade as their girlfriends might be there.

Then there was also the fact that after the service there was a dance in the parish hall. This was the unspoken main attraction, rather than the service itself. The underlying rationale of these dances was, of course, the aspiration that Catholic boys would marry Catholic girls. (How things have changed! Nowadays the expectation might be that Christian boys marry Christian girls, although some parents have to get used to a Catholic boy marrying a Muslim girl.)

I was an altar boy. Girls were not allowed to do this job. In one parish of which I was a member, the very conservative parish pastor surprisingly did have altar girls. He was heavily criticised for this as the Catholic rule book (Canon Law) did not allow it. His bishop was reported to Rome for allowing it. I don't think the bishop was worried as he thought there were more pressing issues than that. Today thankfully, we do have male and female altar servers but misogyny is still very much around.

What was magnified in Catholicism was Mariology, the devotion to Mary (or the study of Mary). This was always a stumbling block for Christians of other denominations. They saw Catholics as worshipping Mary. And they had a point because, too often, devotion to Mary seem to dominate. Let me give one example. If you look at the churches in Dublin, for example, you will see typically two statues, one of Mary and the other of Jesus (the same would apply to many churches in South America and elsewhere as well). Now Christians believe in God as triune, Father, Son and Holy Spirit, yet this is often not obvious looking at the statues and pictures in a Catholic church.

This influenced our teaching as well. Devotions and Mary could dominate. I recall a good-natured, ten-year-old boy in class when I was a young teacher, who thought 'Mother Mary' was the answer to any question he would be asked in a subject called 'religious education'. To any question on this subject, his hand would shoot up and he would offer 'Mother Mary' as the likely answer. He probably had about 50% chance of being correct!

Overall, growing up as a Catholic you learnt that there were rules made by the church, to be obeyed if you wanted to get to heaven. Mass attendance was one such rule. Those who missed Sunday Mass without a really good excuse committed a mortal (big) sin. This could send you to hell. The world was fraught with dangers. One could easily 'fall into' sin. Hence the need for salvation *from* the world. Today's theology has thankfully changed and disagrees with this approach, speaking more holistically of 'salvation *of* the world'.

I grew up in the Catholicism of the 1950 era, of the pre-Vatican II days when we had a very hierarchical, judgmental, devotional institution called the church. Great emphasis was placed on numbers, that is, quantity was better than quality. The numbers going to communion were important, the percentage of Catholics going to church every week was important. Numbers measured the success rate of Catholicism. The theology was severe, full of fear, with God judging all you did during your life. After death, the individual faces judgment, followed by heaven or hell.

One could say that the kind of religion I grew up with was devotionalism, i.e. a religious practice that was given over to devotions of various types, while there was no interest in studying the Bible or discussing theological issues since doctrine was there to be learnt not questioned.

A very 'religious' person was very conscientious about devotions and carried them out with great application. Such a person might say a few rosaries a day, say prayers to their favourite saint, make novenas, have statues of the Sacred Heart and Mary at home, and read religious books that dripped with saccharine sentiment. I was never that type. In fact that kind of spirituality repelled me.

Vatican II (a Church Council, 1962-5) changed much of this kind of church and theology, or at least began to change it. God was loving and compassionate, not all sin was mortal, the church needed to engage in everyday life more and God loves everyone.

Now we have a further change, a paradigm change in fact, with the New Creation Story. Creation started 13.8 billion years ago, as mentioned above, and the human race has evolved only recently in this long history. We are Earthlings and the reality of climate change makes us think of planet Earth as our home and therefore the caring of all creation, humans, animals, flora and fauna is our duty. This implies that I must undergo an 'ecological conversion'. From a theology where saving one's soul was the main objective, one must change to one in which 'saving God's Earth' (or its modern understanding[14] is the highest calling. Quite a jump!

One could summarise this paradigm shift as follows. As regards doctrine, I have experienced a change from learning the teachings/doctrine by heart to acting according to the gospels; from seeing 'saving my soul' as all important to working for the wellbeing and liberation of the whole of creation. As regards attitudes: from blind obedience to authority and the church, to a critical appraisal of institutions like the church and its use of power. The Bible, as well as being divine in origin, was written by human beings and showed the ability to progress its thinking and attitudes. It was certainly not a handbook with answers to all our problems, past and present.

When it comes to devotional practices, there is a change from carrying out religious devotions like novenas, benediction, and saying the rosary, to reflective meditation and engagement in justice issues.

Authority has taken a big hit with the sexual abuse of minors, which has sped up the movement from seeing obedience to authority as the main game to trying to be authentic, transparent and apply the gospel values to daily life. I am trying to move into this way of seeing things. My thinking and practice continues to evolve while I try to meet this challenge.

Talking about devotions and liturgy, one of the great experiences I had regarding liturgy was at Oxford in the UK many years ago. Although I was not given to devotionalism I did appreciate good liturgies. I was staying at the Jesuit-run Campion College on study leave.

I heard that every Sunday evening there was a typical Anglican Evensong at Christ College (founded by Henry VIII) not far from where I was staying. The college is noted for its stunning architecture but I went along for its liturgy. Not surprisingly, I was deeply impressed with the decorum, the beautiful choir singing and prayerful atmosphere during the service.

This is a type of service I never experienced in the Catholic tradition where Sunday evenings was usually either 'rosary and benediction' or 'sermon and benediction', and services were often rushed through with mindless haste. At one time, I recall we had two Dominican priests, actually brothers, who vied for the prize of having the fastest time for saying the Mass. We timed them. The first had a record of 17 minutes while the second beat him with 16 minutes. This was the epoch when the Mass was said in Latin. The expression of 'saying' the mass was indeed accurate since it was seldom 'prayed'.

Parents and politics

It always was a bit of a mystery to me as an adult, why my parents did not talk about politics. Perhaps they did but not in my presence. As my parents came from two different groups in South Africa, the Afrikaans-speaking section and the English-section, they must have had some discussions on certain matters. Yet since they decided to get married, they must have ironed out any potential problems before they took the big step.

My father was brought up a Calvinist, or more specifically, as it is called in South Africa, the Dutch Reformed Church, When he became a Catholic, he was alienated from his large family, except for one married sister as far as I know. This sister and her husband had received friendship and help from the Catholic nuns in the village where they lived as a young couple, and as a result, knew from their interaction with Catholics that they were not all bad!

This might have had a huge impact on my father because throughout his life he worked for better understanding among members of Christian denominations. Today this vision has expanded globally to include a better understanding among all religions (Christian, Jews, Muslim, Hindu, etc.) and atheists.

In the era of sectarianism, we all grew up fed on the copious diet of popular myths about 'the other'. I was told, for example, that in *Die Apostoliese Kerk* (The Apostolic Church, a breakaway in 1955, from the New Apostolic Church – a kind of Pentecostal church), they held a service in which they called down the Holy Spirit. At the appropriate moment young boys who were on the roof of the church, removed some tiles and let a dove in who became the Holy Spirit for the congregation!

My father did a lot of writing and translating related to his work for the magazine *Die Brug* and other publications. He was aware of some of the mistakes churches made preaching the gospel and seeking conversions. He liked to remind us of the dangers of translating from one language to another, and cited the following example. In Afrikaans, the word for manure is *'mis'*. Many black South Africans knew a little Afrikaans so they would have understood the word *mis*. So when the white Catholic missionaries preached to the blacks in Afrikaans and told them the importance of the *Heilige mis* (Holy Mass), they were understandably shocked and dumbfounded about this 'holy manure'.

We also were told that the straight-laced Calvinists were told to stay at home on Sundays after church, draw the curtains and read their Bibles. This was undoubtedly a caricature, but one thing I could not work out was why the Dutch Reformed Church – which had Afrikaans as their language – would have a Scottish preacher of note, the Reverend Andrew Murray (1828-1917) who, although born in Graaff Reinet, South Africa, trained at the University of Aberdeen in Scotland. No one told me that Calvinism was rife in Scotland!

Among the many myths about Catholics were some conspiracy theories. One was that South Africa should not allow immigrants from Italy, Spain and Portugal because they were Catholic countries and the Pope was trying to increase the total Catholic population in South Africa so that they could dominate. (That theory did not take into account the actual statistics!).

Nuns were evil people who might kidnap your child. The pope was the anti-Christ. Catholics were referred to as the 'Roomse gevaar', which meant 'the Roman Danger'. They were dangerous because of their doctrines, (particularly the Marian ones, that is, the ones relating to Mary, the mother of Jesus) but also because they tried to convert others to their church. Although some Protestants circulated evil stories about Catholics, some Catholics responded in kind.

As a Christian, my father was convinced of the need for asking for forgiveness, from God and from each other. (On reflection, forgiveness is central to Christianity.) When I was about eleven or twelve, I joined with a few friends in roughing up a companion whom we thought was a bit of a 'sissy'. It was at night at the school after band practice. Some polishing equipment for the concrete verandahs was left lying around, so we used that to polish the lad. Well, the boy's parents got to hear about it and must have complained to my parents. So on a Sunday morning, my dad took me with him to visit the family and apologise. My father was not angry; nor did he give me a telling-off on how to behave. He just showed me what to do. That lesson was more powerful than any lecture could have been.

Later in life, I have often witnessed with some great dismay that otherwise good Christians are not able to forgive. Constantin Meurier's strikingly compassionate sculpture of *The Prodigal Son* which Caroline and I visited in Museum Leuven, reminds us of this truth in a striking way.

The Prodigal Son by Constantin Meunier (1831-1905)

As children, we were given little chores to do around the house. We often complained about these but did them nevertheless. The rationale was that 'there are no slaves in this house' and all had to pitch in. For my brothers and me, it was often shopping on our bicycle or polishing the porch, or making the coal fire for baths (an electrical 'geyser' came later).

I also remember that if the rain was threatening, I was asked to take my father's raincoat with me on the bicycle and meet his train at the local station in the late afternoon. My mother was very thoughtful and caring about this. My father was the only breadwinner for the family, and she, having grown up in the aftermath of WWII, was very conscious that to have and hold a job was vital for survival.

As far as I know, my mother never considered looking for a paid job once she married. It was common for a wife to stay at home. Moreover, my mother had five children to look after! In those days, it was possible for a family to survive on one salary while paying off a mortgage. Today it is not. In my case, it meant that my mother was always at home when we came back from school – many mothers today cannot do this.

In many cases today, both parents have to work to survive financially. School children returning to an empty house can create certain problems which challenges the assumption that modern life is forever getting better.

Although we believed that blacks and white were equal before God, we did not take any actions regarding the incidents and laws of unfair discrimination we saw around us. That blacks could not share the same beaches with us, or same trains, buses, or schools did not seem to worry us. We seem to accept the government's doctrine of *Apartheid* (since

1948) that the races must live apart. Anyone who took up issues of social justice in the country were quickly labelled as 'communists' or 'agitators' of trouble. To be called a communist in those days was the ultimate insult. Anyone who rocked the national boat was a national security risk.

In retrospect, it is interesting how bogeymen/myths have their day and are then reborn with a new name. Communists became agitators, trouble makers, or terrorists in a later era. One notes that being called a 'socialist' still persist today in some countries (Australia, USA) as the ultimate lowlife although the meaning of the word has various definitions. I like to challenge people by saying that the early Christians were communists. That is normally sufficient to get a lively discussion going.

Growing up in such an atmosphere was definitely affected by the prejudices and lies around me. I recall when I went to Europe how a friend of mine from the English College, Rome, used to challenge me as to the unfair allocation of educational funds to blacks compared with whites in South Africa. Initially I was inclined to defend the government position by denying the reality, but later thought over the matter and slowly began to change my thinking.

This was furthered by studying the social teachings of the Catholic Church – teachings that many have termed 'the best kept secret of the Church'. Catholics often hear about doctrines relating to issues such as abortion, euthanasia and sexual ethics, but rarely about social teachings such as a living wage, the right to work, the right to form unions, teachings about justice, racism, misogyny, and human rights. I will return to this topic below.

Growing up in South Africa in the Apartheid era had its peculiarities. The following episode relates to the state security in South Africa. Let me fill you in. In South Africa, The Bureau for State Security was known as BOSS for short. It was the main state intelligence agency from 1969 to 1980. It reported directly to the Prime Minister.

I remember the situation in the 1970s, having returned from Europe, I was teaching ethics at St Joseph's Scholasticate, Cedara, KwaZulu (previously called the province of Natal). The tertiary college had white and students 'of colour'. This was against the law, but somehow the government tolerated it. I was told by staff that there were probably some 'plants' among the students and to be careful what you said because it would be reported. I never found out who the plants were but I also was never subjected to any harassment. The secretary of the college told me she was approached by a BOSS agent to inform on what was happening at the college. She declined the offer.

In the light of this information, I was quick to dispose of a book I possessed and which was prohibited by the South African government. The book was Mao's *The Little Red Book* which I had used in doing my doctoral studies into the topic of 'work'. (The book was a collection of statements and speeches by the leader of the communist party Mao-Zedong.) Discovery of such a book in our house would have been sufficient evidence that I was a communist!

While doing further research at the University of Natal on the topic of 'Racial Equality', I was surprised to find that some books on my topic were available in the university library but had to be read in the library and could not be taken home. 'Weird', I thought. It is truly amazing how some dictatorial governments think they can control what people think and read, especially now, years on, with all the digital possibilities.

The Catholic Church is no stranger to prohibited books. Despots have banned or burnt books since time immemorial. The autocratic Chinese Emperor Qin Shihuang (221- 210 BCE) was quick 'to burn the books and bury the scholars' as his way of repressing intellectual freedom.[15] The Nazi party in the 1930s did not hesitate to burn the books of communists like Marx, Thomas Mann and Georg Glaser.

The Catholic Church, in its turn, stubbornly resisted the Enlightenment and forbade certain books. This list of banned books was known as the *Index*. It was frequently updated and the latest edition was that of 1948. The list was only definitively abolished in 1966 by Pope Paul VI but that narrow frame of mind often lingers on.

So having worked in a Catholic College of Education and Catholic University for most of my life, the issue was sure to turn up. It was at the Teachers College where I was Head of the Religious Education Department in the late 1970s.

The Principal of the College invited me to meet with a visitor to the college (whose name I cannot recall). In the course of the discussion, the name of the dissident Swiss theologian, Hans Küng, came up. At this point, the Principal turned to me and said: 'We wouldn't have any of his books in our library, would we?' I said I was not sure but I would check it out. I think the Principal was very diplomatic on this issue because he never got back to me to find out the answer. (Küng was one of my cherished theologians!)

By the way, one of the most valued customs of university life is the opportunity to have study leave, or a sabbatical every so many years. This is a great opportunity to travel to other universities and observe new ways of how they teach and research and get ideas that you may integrate into your work. Some would say it 'broadens the mind'.

What I found utterly odd was the fact that, in applying for such a sabbatical, one has to go to great lengths to justify all the travel and visits (which I accept), but when you return to your university, and submit your report, no one reacts. At least that was my experience. Perhaps no one reads the reports. But what a waste of time and money if insights are not shared!

Growing up Catholic teaches you much along the way. One is that the Catholic Church has a definite way of handling difficult issues when they don't want to take action. They simply let the issue run dead. This was my experience when Rome asked a certain archbishop to investigate a theologian's work.

The archbishop, a friend of the theologian, not wanting to rock the boat, simply did not reply to the Roman letter. This was discovered when a second accusation of being a heretic surfaced twenty years later and the original Roman letter was found in the file! Apparently Rome did not follow up on the matter.

Given the vast number of Catholic bishops in the world (about five thousand now), it is not surprising if the bureaucrats cannot follow up all their letters! I am happy to note that Pope Francis does not make heresy-hunting his number one objective (he has re-written the aims of the Congregation for the Doctrine of the Faith). In the past, however, being a heresy-hunter was a sure pathway to promotion within the Catholic Church system.

Clashes with authority can have a humorous side. I am thinking of the following incident. In 1973, on returning to South Africa by the *Edinburgh Castle*, we faced the authorities in Cape Town at the docks. In my hand luggage, the official noticed a book entitled, *The Political Christ*.[16] The book was by a well-known author, Alan Richardson. The official was happy with 'Christ' but the other word bothered him. Their juxta-positioning raised suspicions. He now faced a dilemma so he wisely took the book to his supervisor for a second opinion as you would do with a serious symptom. Should he allow it or not? After a short pause, the vote went my way and I got to keep my book!

Capitalism and socialism

In growing up, Catholic issues of justice rise to the surface sooner or later. The above story of politics and religion is one such incident. (I will have more to say on the church in the next chapter.)

In Catholicism, if we look carefully, we find a strong thread of issues related to justice. It is known as the 'social teachings' of the Catholic Church. Many Catholics have never come across them. The issues received great attention with the rise of the industrial revolution in the eighteenth century. I have had the opportunity to read up in this area, but for the average Catholic it is probably unknown territory.

It deals with issues like a living wage, strikes, trade unions, poverty, distributive and restorative justice, essential services, democracy and socialism, taxation, human rights, ownership relative and absolute. You may ask what is the relevance of all these ideas today? The connection is clear. Today we have the ever-increasing gap between rich and poor; a lack of housing, rising cost of living and low wages, lack of work opportunities (think of the economic refugees in Europe and North America), human rights, the need for restorative justice. Underlying all these is often a lack of searching for the common good.

Socialism is often dismissed without analysing what it means, liberalism is embraced without critical reflection. There is also neglect on the part of church leaders to educate congregations on changes in teachings and emphases after the council known as Vatican II (1962-5). Leaders seemed happy to leave congregations uninformed.

Today, many are re-considering their adherence to a church because of the lack of transparent church reform. This, I think, will lead to decrease in numbers although church groups differ enormously across the globe in terms of what they believe and reject.

What gave me some hope of reform in the recent past, was the incident called the *Pact of the Catacombs* when, in 1965 a number of bishops (42), inspired by a suggestion of bishop Helder Camara, gathered in the catacombs of St Domitilla on the Via Appia in Rome during the council, and pledged themselves to focus on the poor and needy, social justice and the lay apostolate. Forty years later, there was a repetition of this pledge by a number of bishops.

This story shows me that there are still bishops who can see that the church has lost its way to some extent, and needs to reform ... or die out. This is exactly what others are saying. Belief in reform of the Catholic Church requires strong faith. This faith has been challenged by the slowness of reform since Vatican II. Impatience is growing. A recent book (2023) authored by seven women theologians (French and Italian; editor, Isabelle de Gaulmyn) says it all: The title is: *Se réformer ou mourir* (Reform or die out).

We need to keep on insisting on reform in structures, attitudes, teachings, and mission, in order to survive and thrive. This is my firm belief.

This does not overlook the empathy which needs to be shown leaders like the ordained, who do not find easy changes from a dictatorial role to collaboration. The change from pastor-centred to community-centred is not easy. (As teachers we were instructed about moving from a teacher-centred model to a pupil-centred one.) Many find it too much and if there are programs designed to help them, it is not apparent. Over the last forty years, I have only come across one or two pastors/priests who have shown an ability to collaborate rather than dictate.

One major problem is that many Catholics are happy with the infantilisation of the laity. Let 'Father' decide. They are not encouraged to speak out. They are told what to do. Younger ones might be different especially after the sex scandals.

Reform has made me look more closely at the way the church spends money on buildings and things rather than on people. There is also a need for unions to defend rights of people, e.g. trying to fire a worker without a sound reason, or paying workers below-poverty wages. There is a need too to see parishes as communities not owned by an ordained person but belonging to the community. This brings in the question of power and how it is used or misused.

All the above is part of the struggle against individualism, selfishness, greed, wealth, claims to absolute ownership, and wanting individual rights to prevail over collective rights. The struggle is continuous and difficult. However, I believe we must not give up.

In the above section, I have covered a lot of ground with references to my religious background. Now, in what follows, let me turn more specifically to one of the main protagonists in my story, the Catholic Church.

4

Holy Mother and Unholy Father

In this chapter, I want to comment on some ideas on the church. By 'church' I mean Catholic Church in which I have spent my lifetime, although much of what I say applies to other Christian churches as well. Over the years, my understanding of what 'church' should be has evolved.

For some, the idea of church means at least a community of people, and although the numbers attending a Christian church is decreasing, the value of people getting together and forming a community is still a worthwhile and necessary goal for many. I think it will continue to be strong because it is part of being human to form communities to give each other mutual support and to communicate with others.

As I see it, for many today belonging to a club is important. The focus of the belonging is very varied. It could be football, netball, bowling, women's association, chess, vintage cars, golf, bird watching, philosophy, rock or classic music. It is a basic human need to belong to group like a club.

Religious communities (churches) tap into the need to belong to a club but they go further and make spiritual well-being the main focus. Thus, I see belonging to a church as a very human activity as well as a spiritual one.

So why are churches in some parts of the world in decline? The answer might have more to do with the way these communities are being run, that is, their institutional face. This would correlate with the general disaffection of many towards institutions today.

One of the reasons for this disaffection is that people see institutions as caught up with themselves, rather than with the service they purport to offer society. I recall one local bank advertising that their 'customers come first', while progressively closing down local branches!

Another name for this is being 'self-referential', that is, always referring everything to self, to one's own image and interests.

The self-referential church

Today, I see the above more clearly. In the past growing up, I always sensed that the high-ups, that is, the office holders in the church were self-consumed. Observing some people in the church, I was convinced that many seemed focused on themselves, be it building grand edifices, or raising money, or driving big cars and living in palatial presbyteries.

Focusing on money was one give-away. As I mentioned above in Chapter 2, I only once lived in a parish where the serving pastors said they would have nothing to do with the money and would leave that to the finance committee. They never preached on money, they never implored people to give more, they stuck to preaching the gospel.

I need to add that these pastors belonged to a religious community (the Spiritan Fathers in fact), that is, they were not diocesan pastors. I say this because there often seems to me to be a qualitative difference between members of religious orders and pastors who go through a diocesan seminary.

I sense that the term 'Holy Mother Church' is often used in some Catholic circles to refer to the Catholic Church. It suggests the image of 'mother' who is both caring and holy – someone who only wants the best for you and will always look after you.

Some insightful person has quipped that he did not have any problems with 'Holy Mother Church – it was 'Unholy Father Church' that was the problem, thus signalling the origin of problems in patriarchy, misogyny, clericalism and arrogance – the antithesis of holy and caring. I will tease out these ideas in the story that follows.

I know that my father was part of a group in the 1950s called Catholic Action (strongly influenced in 1912 by Joseph Cardijn, a Belgian Cardinal known for his social activism), about which I know very little except that they tried to take some practical steps in particular cases of justice; and promoted social justice issues in general. As a small boy, all you knew was that your dad had gone out to a meeting and would be home later. As I said above, my father was part of a movement of *rapprochement* between Catholics and the Dutch Reformed Church. This continued for many years during my young adulthood.

I can recall reading some of what my father wrote and how he constantly used the term the 'Kingdom of God'. His upbringing was within the Dutch Reformed Church and they are very biblical as the reformers were. So I wondered about this constant reference to 'the Kingdom of God'.

Thinking back on this, Catholics would have used the term *The Church*, meaning the Catholic Church. Growing up a Catholic in the 1950s with a string of authoritarian popes like Pius X, Pius XI and Pius XII, it was no wonder that the concept of church loomed large in our religion.

The church authorities were to be obeyed. They specified what the church laws (rather than the Beatitudes) were and how they were to be kept. Any exceptions to these laws could only be granted by the highest of authorities and under very special circumstances. The church said you had to go to church every Sunday and that had to be obeyed. Anyone who did not was frowned upon. This introduced the attitude of being judgmental, with which, I am afraid, we grew up.

Regarding the Sunday rule of attendance, it never occurred to us that Jesus never mentioned this rule in the gospel. Growing up, I had to discover that there was no such rule for Anglicans, Methodists, Baptists and other Christians. I was further educated by my Ukrainian friend who said their approach was that it was a privilege to go to 'the divine mysteries' on a Sunday, not an obligation. This motivation seemed a nobler way to see Sunday worship.

I can add here the manifestation of arrogance when the Catholic Church assumes a role of trying to say where and when God can act. I am thinking of admission to the Lord's table, called 'communion'. In many Christian churches, it is left to the individual to make up their minds whether they go to receive the host or not. After all, Christ commanded his followers to receive the consecrated bread and wine. But in the Catholic tradition, the Church has been rigid in barring some from reception in an attempt to control God's action.

I am not denying that a church needs to regulate the way it worships, but in the case of reception of communion, I do not think the Catholic Church has found the balance. On the other hand, I know that some Christians (belonging to another denomination), who attend a Catholic Eucharist will take communion because they feel it is all right. This is the way it felt for me when I received communion at the Anglican Christ Church Cathedral in Dublin in 2001.

It was only much later in life when I read Hans Küng's book, *The Church* (1967), that I saw more clearly how the Catholic Church had made the church the focal point of religion instead of seeing the Kingdom of God as the central idea. His insights have helped me relativise the church.

Pope Francis referred to that focus on the church as the 'self-referential church' – always drawing attention to itself instead of the gospel. To this day, I believe some bishops do not grasp this point. We all know where that ended up with the sex and money scandals, abuse, clericalism, authoritarianism and the lack of humility which often expressed itself in the inability of leaders to admit making a mistake and to apologise. The fact that some bishops still live in luxurious 'palaces' says it all.

Too much focus on self, either as an individual or collectively as Church, is unhealthy. Here is where using the term 'Kingdom of God' can give the Catholic Church an opening to others, be more inclusive. If the term 'Kingdom of God' (which is gospel language) is the focal point, then dialoguing with other faiths, such as Islam, Hinduism, Buddhism, etc., becomes easier since they all reflect some dimensions of what Christians mean by Kingdom of God. Thus the term 'Kingdom of God' gives Christians the possibility to dialogue with other faiths, whereas the over-emphasis on the 'Catholic Church' can be, and has been, exclusive.

Sexual abuse and the church

Growing up in the era of 1940-1960, I never heard of sexual abuse and, even if I did, I would not have known what it was. Thus I cannot comment about the frequency of cases. I did have some idea of domestic violence because I saw it. One of our friends would never bring us into his house (we waited at the gate) because his father was perpetually drunk and threatened his son from time to time. That taught us that not all households were safe places. Perhaps I was lucky but I never came across any teacher, pastor or adult who made me feel in any way uncomfortable from a sexuality point of view. So when cases became public in the 1990s, I was as shocked as others.

About this time, cases were coming to the fore in Australia. When many cases were in the press, on the radio, on TV and nothing was said in our parish, either inside or outside the church, I took action. I was a reader at the Saturday Vigil Mass. On this particular day I went to the sacristy to check my reading against the translation as was the custom. Sometimes, the translation one used at home to prepare the reading was not the same as in the book used at the Eucharist. In any case, the parish pastor, myself, the acolyte or senior server, and altar boys were there in the sacristy.

I said to the pastor that something needs to be said to the congregation about the sexual abuse as it is all over the media and we have said nothing (as if we lived in a different world)! Well, all hell was let loose! The pastor went apoplectic with rage about how the media causes all this fuss and creates all the problems!! On and on he went blaming everyone else. Such fury we had not seen from the parish pastor either before or since. I thought to myself: I have touched a nerve here, but it is not the media's fault. So nothing was said at his service, and on went the farce of pretence.

I must say that I had heard nothing regarding sexual abuse of minors involving the Christian Brothers in Australia. I was thus surprised at the number of cases when the report came out as a result of the Royal Commission of Enquiry. Nor had I ever heard of any cases regarding them in South Africa.

Now, decades later, after many investigatory commissions in various countries, we know who was responsible, although the institutional church has generally handled the whole sad saga badly. On the positive side, on 13 November 2021, Pope Francis publicly thanked the media for the role they played in revealing cases of sexual abuse. Pope Francis said journalists had a mission to explain the world, to make it less obscure, to make those who live in it less fearful and grateful for what it did have. The pope added: '(I) thank you for what you tell us about what is wrong in the Church, for helping us not to sweep it under the carpet, and for the voice you have given to the abuse victims'.[17]

One of the things that I noticed was that the patterns of behaviour of people in authority in the church were paralleled in the secular world. In 2021, the cases of sexual abuse (committed over the previous twenty years or more) in women's soccer/football and in children's swimming associations came to light in Australia.

The coaches were quietly moved to other swimming clubs and nothing was done, just like offending parish pastors were quietly moved to other parishes where they continued to abuse children. When perpetrators were confronted, they denied any wrongdoing. The administrators of sporting associations, like church authorities (bishops), tended to do nothing about the cases that came to their attention. They also had supreme power over the children they coached or taught like parish pastors and bishops do with regard to their parishioners.

These institutions (sporting associations, churches) do not have the checks and balances that need to be in place. Swimming or football coaches need to have someone overseeing their activities. Bishops and pastors have too much power with few or no checks.

Since these early days of the disclosures, a practice called 'Listening Circles' has been introduced as a way for people to process what is happening to them and their churches. People have been reluctant to speak. They have been shocked into silence. In some cases they have retreated into a determined denial. Many left the church before these circles became available. I am afraid the institutional Church was too late in responding.

When I hear of all the cases of sexual abuse of minors within the Catholic Church today, particularly of people you know, I often consider myself lucky to have escaped that kind of fate. I particularly think of an incident that makes me shudder even today.

In the late 1940s, living in a remote, God-forsaken town called Mafeking (now called 'Mahikeng' meaning 'the place of rocks') in northwestern Cape Province near the border of Botswana, we had a good parish pastor who will go unnamed in this account, although I do remember this name. Part of his duty was to go to a mission station run by nuns some distance into the 'veld' (or 'bush') to preside at the Eucharist. This pastor asked my parents if I could go with him to open all the gates of the farms he had to drive through to get to the mission station. The pastor would spend the night there at the mission and I would be altar boy for him in the morning at Mass.

My parents agreed to this request although I was probably only eight or nine years old. I don't think I was afraid to go. I was probably fairly neutral about the whole thing. There was no great excitement in store. What happened was that I slept in the same room as the pastor but in a different bed. All I can remember is falling asleep while the pastor was still moving around the room. I am pleased to say that nothing untoward happened, but when I think of it retrospectively in the light of what we all know now, I shudder.

Of course, my parents knew nothing of pastors sexually abusing minors then as it was all kept in the dark. We grew up quite unaware of these kinds of crimes and assumed (because we accepted clericalism) that pastors would never do anything as terrible as that. (Fast forward forty years and some of my local parishioners would not believe that our parish pastor was having affairs and children with some of his parishioners. Many parishioners could not believe that a pastor would do such things.)

Thinking about this issue, I am convinced that as far as the Catholic Church goes, the power of the bishop and the parish pastor must be restricted. They have got to be responsible to someone, or some group of elders, at hand. To perpetuate the monarchical model of power has got to be rejected in favour of a model of accountability and responsibility. This will be a big obstacle for the Catholic Church as the bishops and pastors have the power at the moment and we all know that people in positions of power rarely willingly forfeit any of their power. It normally has to be wrested from them.

Possessing power can easily feed into the clerical mindset which allows individuals to act unjustly with impunity. Let me cite one example of power abuse, from my own experience. A certain bishop took a disliking to a member (secular priest) of a (Catholic) tertiary college. Although the priest had committed no crime or broken any rules, the bishop was determined to get rid of him. Fortunately for the priest, he was a member of a trade union who supported him. The bishop would have proceeded with the firing were it not for a fellow bishop who warned him that such action would involve the union and a costly court case. The first bishop backed down and the priest remained on staff. This kind of flouting of the rights of working people by the hierarchy, has undermined any moral standing that they had. The same applies to other areas like sexual morality or truth telling.

Having discussed some of the burning issues regarding 'church', let me now turn to the heart of much of our life's journey, namely education. It is time to reflect on some aspects of this part of life.

5

The trick of matric

In the beginning

When I started teaching fulltime at Christian Brothers College, Welkom, Orange Free State in South Africa, I was given a junior class in Primary school that would be the equivalent to Year 3 (about 8/9 years old) in Australia today. On Day One, the jovial principal introduced me to the class and then disappeared.

Later in the day, he called by to see how things were going. He quietly sidled up to me at the front of the class and said *sotto voce*: 'Why don't you open some windows? It is very hot in here!' I was so preoccupied with teaching that I forgot to regulate the air flow as the temperature was rising in the classroom! I must say I often get very absorbed in my teaching to the point that I forget what is happening around me.

I was lucky to have a good, sympathetic and cheerful principal who really cared for his staff. I felt I had his support and that of the staff. Many staff members were my age or a little older and I learnt a lot from them. Year 3 was a good introduction to teaching for me but the next year I taught year 7 (first year of high school) and found that far more to my liking. I found the students could do a lot of independent work and my subjects included Algebra and Geometry – two of my favourite subjects.

Teaching has moved from being teacher-centred to pupil-centred. That is true, but I always tried to emphasise student learning and discovery. I resented the way we, in our last years at high school, were taught how to pass examinations rather than encouraged to discover things. The syllabus and exams ruled the day. Today too, one sees how the final HSC exam can easily tend to subvert true learning.

Discipline was rough and ready when I went through school and continued when I taught, but less so. This was the general practice in all schools not just the Christian Brothers. However, I must say I reckon that many of my teachers should not have become teachers. Some showed what I would now call pathological weaknesses that should have excluded them from the profession. Too much physical punishment, a lack of empathy and a willingness to constantly humiliate students should not be part of classroom education.

In retrospect, I must admit that the teacher training in those days was far too short. In some cases, only one year, and getting in large numbers of trainees was perhaps more important that the quality of the teachers.

I particularly resented the occasion when my older brother's teacher had me summoned into his class to answer a question that my brother could not answer. I think it was in the Latin class. The aim was clearly to humiliate my brother. As it turned out, the stunt nearly backfired on the teacher because I too did not know the answer and had to be given a clue before I got it right.

A subject I feel was neglected in my education was music. As an adult, I am absolutely convinced that some education in music and its appreciation is necessary as an integral part of human development. We had some music lessons in primary school but all I remember is writing down the words of songs from the blackboard and disciplinary trouble in the class with students whose music books were in tatters or lost. I do not recall any pleasure in singing. Perhaps we never got that far! What a lost opportunity!

On a more positive note, I recall an unexpected opportunity I had. The school I attended, CBC Boksburg, was introducing a pipe band. One of the teachers called a meeting during the lunch break and announced they would need drummers and pipers. I put my hand up to become a drummer but the teacher pointed out that as there were many hands up for drummers it might take a long time before you got into the band. The competition would be too great. On the other hand there were only a few hands up for pipers. So I thought: I'll become a piper. On reflection (and with the help of *Ancestry*) there is plenty of Irish and Scottish blood in me that would help me.

The bagpipe teacher was Jim Creighton, who I must say was a good and patient teacher. My theory now, reflecting as an adult, was that Jim Creighton who was the person in charge of the local Caledonian Pipe Band must have approached the school to teach pipers and set up a school pipe band with an eye on recruits for his senior band that played at Boksburg Lake once a month in summer. I say that because that is where I landed up. The reality was that the school band did not play very often, whereas the senior local band played regularly. He was also allowed to have his senior band practice on weekends in the school grounds.

I was not very committed to practising the chanter (the instrument on which one learns) at home. We had some out-rooms at the back to which I was banished because of the noise that pipes made especially when played by a novice!

Jim Creighton, who had a thick Scottish accent, was a shrewd psychologist. He realised that he needed to give us something to look forward to while we toiled away at the practice chanter, so he allowed us to play as soon as possible in the senior band even if we only knew one or two tunes well enough to join in. The secret is you can pretend to play and the public won't know. Just move your fingers and pretend to blow! From Jim's viewpoint, he needed to booster the numbers in his band.

I recall my first unforgettable outing with the senior band. We were asked to play at a parade of the St John's Ambulance Association at Springs, a small town nearby, as I recall. The idea of wearing a kilt, tunic, sporran, spats, etcetera, was exciting. The colours we wore for the senior band were the Hunting Stewart kilt, while for the school we wore the Irish orange and green outfit which I did not think as impressive as the Hunting Stewart tartan (a green-based tartan with shades of blue).

On the day, we turned up and got into formation. I noticed that the bag (of the bagpipes) was not filling up with air as it should. I blew harder until I went blue in the face, but still had no feeling of the bag firming up with air. I thought: why is it so difficult today? Was it the public occasion? So when the band started playing *Skye Boat Song* while the troops were being inspected, I was unable to make any noise but just pretended to play. The next Tuesday night at band practice I was relieved when Jim Creighton inspected my bagpipes and discovered a hole in the bag!

During this period of my life (10 to 14 years old), I was also a boy scout. It meant Friday evening meetings in the church hall. We were divided into patrols. I rose to the job of patrol leader. It was a bit like a little army. I was the leader and I had four or five younger boys in my patrol.

I learnt many skills during this period. Weekend outdoor camps taught one how to pitch and strike a tent (a big heavy canvass one not like the light-weights of today!). We would travel to the campsite with all our gear on the back of a truck. Invariably one of the scouts would fall over and accidentally sit on the pawpaw which had been earmarked for desert after Sunday lunch!

At scouts, we also learned to light a fire, cook a meal, dig a dunny, apply basic first aid, learn to tie knots, to communicate with semaphore and do some elementary decoding. If you wanted to pursue the proficiency badges there were additional skills you could acquire and qualify for the Second or First Class badge. All this in an era when there were no mobile phones or digital games to distract one!

Once a year, we entered the Boy Scout competition camp for our district. This camp lasted a weekend and, during this time, our skills were tested in competition with other patrols from different scout troops. I recall one occasion when I let down the team. I was patrol leader. Our cook had great trouble in getting the evening fire going to cook our food so the evening meal was repeatedly delayed as the fire went out time and again.

After much frustration and not much progress made on cooking anything, we finally ate something roughly and generously described as a meal. By this time it was dark and, as a safety measure, I did not want patrol members going down to the dam in the dark to wash the plates. I ordered them off to bed and to leave the plates unwashed until the morning. It so happened that the inspectors (scout leaders) decided to come around and inspect our plate rack (made of little sticks bound together) and noticed the plates were still dirty. I owned up unrepentantly to the fact, so we were marked down. Actually, to this day, I think my decision was correct.

As children, we learn by watching and imitating others. We mime them. René Girard produced his memetic theory by reflecting on this aspect of learning. Looking back at scouting, I see it as a good example of this miming.

Another incident that I recall goes back to my cricketing days at CBC Boksburg. We were playing a rival team from CBC Pretoria on their home ground. It was the 'under 12' age group. I loved cricket and was able to bowl a bit and liked to bat although not very good at it yet.

I cannot remember the details of the game except that I was called upon to bowl at one stage. I could pitch the ball up quite well and was reasonably accurate. Bowling on the stumps was a rewarding achievement at this age level, because if the batsman missed hitting the ball (which often happened), the ball hit his stumps and he was 'out'. On this particular day, I got three batsmen out with consecutive balls.

This miracle is known in cricket as a 'hat-trick'. Something very unusual – like pulling a rabbit out of a hat. What I never publicised was the fact that this particular ball had lost it shape (through being hammered by the batsman) and when it hit the pitch it went in all unexpected directions, catching the batsman by surprise and forcing the batsman to hit a catch. So I was greatly aided by the misshapen ball. (Had the umpires been more alert, they would have spotted this and sought a more spherical ball.) Needless to say, I was happy to take all the credit for the miracle and be hailed by my team mates.

Other than cricket, which was probably my best sport, I played other games as well. In fact I was keen on all sports, enjoying the exercise and competition. Rugby was the game that all the boys played at school and, although I enjoyed it, I suffered a broken forearm at age sixteen, when a solidly built boy fell on top of me as he tackled me. All the players on the field told me they heard the break but I heard nothing. My arm healed with time, but to this day I cannot straighten my arm completely.

Tennis was less valued by school authorities but that did not stop me playing it. Later, as a young teacher, I played hockey which I thoroughly enjoyed. Swimming was always there but it was self-taught. In fact, most of my games were played without much, or any, coaching.

Most of our teachers were Christian Brothers from Ireland who did not have any coaching in the games we played. I did get some good coaching in rugby but for the rest I had to learn from friends. It was only when I was at Teachers College that I had the grand opportunity of receiving coaching from two ex-MCC cricketers who offered a two-week course at our College. They knew their stuff and I look back on that course with great gratitude. By way of contrast to my experience, today's youngsters in Australia have great opportunities to get excellent coaching in all kinds of sports.

Talking of schooling, here I must add one of the most dramatic incidents any schoolboy could witness while at school.

In about 1952 or 53, our school caught fire. We lived one block away from the school so normally it took me two or three minutes to amble from home to school in the morning. On this particular day around 5pm, my father was in the garden watering when he noticed a huge flume of smoke rising into the sky above where the school was. I saw it too and we rushed off to see what had happened.

The school was having an extension built on at that time. The cause of the fire was unknown. Some thought the attempt to get rid of bees in the new structure might have caused it. Anyway the fire did great damage. I recall some students had tried to salvage their desks but had to leave them at the top of the stairs as the heat was too much.

Of the three firemen on duty that day, one was driving the mayor around, a second was off sick, so the third had to sling a hose over his shoulder and cycle to the scene! When he got there, he could not find the water hydrant which was buried in dirt. So not a good episode for the local fire brigade. My older brother phoned one of his friends in Springs (a township not far from the school) to tell him the good news. However his friend did not believe him and caught the train to school the next morning to confirm the schoolboys' dreams.

After the fire, the classes were distributed to various schools which offered accommodation help. Our class went down to the parish hall where our two classes divided the space in two with the classes back to back. That meant the teachers faced each other standing in front of their class and had to be on their best behaviour.

The class ahead of us in age believed in the aphorism, 'every cloud having a silver lining'. They got two rooms at the local Dominican convent and had the extra thrill and excitement of pretty girls on campus. Boys and girls were carefully timetabled to have breaks at different times, but very soon the boys and girls worked out a system of romantic communications via scribbled notes carefully concealed at various pick-up points in the hedge, rather like drop-off points used by spies. In this way the school fire had some unexpected and welcome consequences!

Matric

When I was at school, the final year was called Standard 10 (preceded by Sub A and Sub B and 9 years.) My last two years at high school were focused on passing the 'matric' exam – short for 'matriculation examination'. It was the big and final test before one stepped into the wider world.

We did not have a choice of subjects. What was on offer for me was basically a classical education. Our languages were simply English, Afrikaans and Latin, The science subjects were Geography, Maths and Science. 'Science' was a combination of Physics and Chemistry.

I disliked Latin because it seems pointless to learn a dead language. What irked me too was the method of teaching it. It was mainly through learning Latin vocabulary daily and if you could not give a correct answer, you probably got a smack with the strap. Latin was weaponised by the teacher to control the students.

Much of the content seemed irrelevant. We were asked to translate sentences like 'the farmer's daughter married the sailor's son' which did not connect with our world. A use of comic strips and jokes in Latin might have stimulated our interest. Too much emphasis was placed on grammar (*Allen's Latin Grammar* in those days) on declensions, conjugations and prepositions, rather than on communication.

The argument that learning Latin helped you with English grammar was not persuasive as one could simple focus more time on English if Latin were dropped. Furthermore, Caesar's Gallic Wars did not enthuse us, once we knew that 'all Gaul was divided into three parts', and that the Helvetti and Vercingetorix were on a hiding to nothing against Julius Caesar, the focus on the grammar of each word in Latin killed off the storyline. The same applied to Ovid's poetry.

South Africa being a bilingual country at that time, Afrikaans was obligatory which was sensible for good communication. However, a little knowledge can be dangerous. Our neighbour only knew a little Afrikaans. She wanted to tell her domestic helper (an African of colour) not to light the fire, saying: 'moenie lieg nie'! Well, the domestic was aghast with surprise and shock because the lady of the house had actually told her, 'don't tell lies'.

I loved Geography because I could learn about other countries and study maps. I loved Maths as well and would spend time out of school hours attempting tricky maths problems which, thankfully, had the correct solutions at the end of the book. Physics was intriguing but in this subject and in Chemistry we never had a laboratory in which to do the experiments. I still feel cheated about not having that practical experience. I feel that science and all education should inspire us to be 'awe hunters' as some have named it.

In retrospect, with the exception of English (I loved the poetry, especially poems from the *Living Tradition*, a textbook we used), I feel that we were taught excellently to do well in the exams, as distinct from being encouraged to think critically and investigate issues.

We were never offered history which turned out to my advantage. Let me explain. When at university doing an arts degree, I thought I would try history as a filler-in to make up my total points for the degree. I tried history for a year, liked it, and did so well with my results that I proceeded to make it a co-major with English. I found that all the history I had to read was fresh and interesting for me, whereas those students who did history in high school were sick and tired of doing the causes of the French Revolution for the umpteenth time!

If I think about which teacher made the most lasting impression on me, it would have to be Professor W. H. Gardner, who was our lecturer at university. His enthusiasm for his topic – be it the poetry of Gerald Manly Hopkins or Shakespeare – was contagious. At this time of my life, I saw my first professionally acted Shakespearean play and my eyes were opened as to how good it could be.

Education has many high and low points. One way or another, we work our way through it all, matriculate, and emerge as an adult. Sometimes, there are hairy moments and at others, there are rewards. To the rewards we now turn.

One reward for me was an exchange program with a scholar from Trinity College, John May. This was in 2001. I am not sure where I got the idea from, but I thought it would be worth having a try. I was dubious about the red tape involved and wondered if many scholars gave up on these exchanges because of excessive red tape. But for me this proved not to be the case.

After a few unsuccessful attempts (one from a philosopher in Vienna where I would have to teach in German, which I was unable to do), I found someone at Trinity College

Dublin, who was keen to exchange. I then approached my university administration to see if they would agree. To my surprise, they did and from there the pathway was straightforward although at one stage I did have to wait for a long time to get some response or other.

Dublin was familiar to me. Some years earlier, on a trip to Dublin, I had visited the world-famous Chester Beatty Library near Dublin Castle. Other than seeing the library and its holdings, I wanted to ask about using copies of some ancient texts that they had. The librarian was very welcoming and I was able to secure copies of fragments of ancient texts of Mark's, Matthew's and John's Gospels for use in a book on scripture which I and a colleague were writing. Fragments from an ancient text of John's Gospel appear on the cover of the book, *Studying the Gospels*.[18]

Back to the exchange program. The contract was simple. I would move to the Irish School of Ecumenics (ISE) within Trinity College, and teach the workload that my exchange scholar normally took and he would take mine in Sydney. This would go on for one term, from September to December. Our own universities would continue to pay us our salaries. This arrangement suited both of us and it meant that Caroline and I could go to Dublin in the autumn and sightsee parts of Ireland before the teaching began.

Blackrock is a suburb of Dublin where I stayed during my time teaching at the ISE. On Saturday mornings, I would do my shopping which entailed walking to the shops and then carrying back what I had purchased. I had no car during that stay which suited me as it was within walking distance of the ISE. On occasions on a Saturday, I would see the crowds walking to Lansdowne Road Stadium (since replaced by the Aviva Stadium) to watch the All Blacks or some visiting team play Ireland.

I will leave the sightseeing part for later and here reflect on the teaching. All the teaching was at postgraduate level, which was a change for me as I usually did both pre- and post-graduate courses back home.

One comment I have is that my teaching load was 5 or 6 hours a week which gave me good time to read and prepare lectures. Back in Australia I was teaching about 14 hours a week which is much too much if one is to keep up with reading and do some research as well. This is part of the battle for resources and finance that goes on in every university. Too often, money considerations outweigh academic ones.

I have always liked postgraduate teaching because you are dealing with adults who have life experience, whereas the undergraduates have very little. And in addition to being all postgraduate students, there was also a great diversity of cultures from Europe, North America, Africa, and South East Asia and elsewhere. This makes for a rich variety of minds and hearts opening a rich sources of learning for everyone.

At the ISE, learning opportunities included lectures, tutorials, seminars, research, excursions, book launches and social events. Irrespective of where you were, or what you were doing, one of the dominant topics which always seem to crop up was *colonialism*. This was not surprising as it reflected the *zeitgeist* which continues to demand attention.

My stay in Ireland was memorable in every respect. Students and staff were kind, friendly and forthcoming. One of my amusing recollections was the discussion I had with research students at Maynooth seminary. The group of students was mixed in terms of gender and profession. It was a pleasant, relaxed atmosphere with wine served at the back of room while the seminar pro ceded. I was surprised at this. Perhaps the atmosphere was too relaxed. As the evening went on, the discussion was becoming increasingly strident so I was glad to declare the seminar closed at a certain point. One of the students was kind enough to drive me back to Blackrock that night.

I decided – when planning the trip to the ISE – that it might be a good idea to take a few of those strange instruments called boomerangs, and see if any students wanted to learn how to throw them. My first problem was that I myself did not know how to throw them. A colleague of mine who knew the art of boomerang throwing kindly offered to give me a crash course in the method of throwing them. I worked hard at this for a few months and could claim at least a 'Pass' category in boomerang throwing. I bought four or five to take with me.

The students responded enthusiastically to my offer to show them how to throw a boomerang in an open field next to the college in Milltown (the ISE was at Milltown before it moved into the city campus) during lunchtime. Fortunately there was a strong wind that day so that the boomerangs were helped on their return journey. The students were delighted and shared their boomerang-throwing stories around. The next day I was quietly approached by the administrative staff of the college who asked if they too could have a boomerang class during a lunchtime break. I was only too happy to oblige.

On another occasion, I attended a Mass at the Church of Ireland cathedral in Dublin, called Christchurch. It has a complicated history but here are some pointers. It was established about 1030 CE and, after the Reformation, became Church of Ireland in1541. Today St Mary's Pro-Cathedral is the seat of Catholic archbishop of Dublin.

Christchurch is very imposing and a beautiful Gothic building. If I recall correctly, the occasion I attended was the feast of Christ the King. The main celebrant was a Church of Ireland archbishop and the preacher was a Catholic Augustinian priest! A very ecumenical service. The experience was such that I felt compelled to receive Communion there.

While teaching at the ISE, a commemorative service was held in the impressive and packed Trinity College Chapel to reflect on those Irish students of Trinity who had died in the 9/11 disaster (the attack on the tower in New York in 2001). Surprisingly, I was asked to give the reflection. I did so, bearing in mind that not all the victims were Christians, much less Catholic. Other than being deeply privileged to be asked, I found the preparation of the reflection a big challenge. What could one say? What consolation can one offer? Eventually, for the reflection, I fixed on the theme of needing to re-frame the incident if we are to move forward with our grief.

Thanks to the generosity of John May and his wife Margret, I was able to use their apartment while in Dublin. There were a number of townhouses build next to each other. Life was very comfortable there although there was one moment of anxiety which I recall with unease.

It was a cold evening in autumn and I was cooking my evening meal. Not surprisingly, sausages were on the menu. I proceeded to grill them while attending to the vegetables. I must have neglected the trusty sausages for a while because the next thing I heard was the fire alarm going off hysterically. The heavy smoke in the kitchen was a give-away. I thought I must switch this shrieking alarm off before it upsets the neighbours, but where is the switch? I looked frantically around the kitchen and stairwell but saw no switch. What shall I do?

I know. I will ask a neighbour because surely they have similar fire alarms. So I flung open the front door and rushed out only to notice that the alarm stopped abruptly as the cold night air swept into the apartment and rushed around kitchen. Well, that solved the problem! No neighbours disturbed. No damage done.

The above stories give some insight into the weird and wonderful world of education Now it is time to move in and look at some unexpected events in life in general.

6
By the skin of my teeth

I will now change the focus of my story and recount some hair-raising incidents. I recall an outing with friends while living in Mafeking. I was about 9 years old. One of our favourite activities was to go into the veld (bush) and observe or shoot birds and set traps for 'rooibekkies' (small birds with a red beak). My older brother had a friend who had an air rifle. This kind of air rifle shot small pellets which were dangerous enough to kill a bird.

The three of us, plus two other friends, went out into the veld on this occasion to shoot birds with only one rifle. On the way home, we were walking along a dirt road in two rows. The second row was myself, my brother and others, walking at some distance behind the first row which was the owner of the air rifle and a friend.

My brother had the rifle and was holding it in his right hand pointing downwards towards the ground. He also unfortunately had his finger on the trigger. As we walked he began swinging his right arm with the rifle in a forward and backward movement. At a certain moment he must have swung too much and then tried to rein in the swing of the rifle using his finger. He fired a shot unintentionally and shot the owner of the rifle (who was walking ahead of him) in his arm near the elbow. Well, you can imagine the panic as we rushed our friend to his house to tell his mother what had happened!

The victim was taken to the hospital and the pellet removed without any permanent damage done. I know our parents went to see the victim's parents and that was the last I heard about the affair.

Bombs away

Another lucky escape comes to mind. I was aged about 12 years old and we were living at Boksburg, not that far from Johannesburg. We had a friend who lived opposite us, Ian, who was older than me and about the same age as my older brother. I hung around them as younger brothers tend to do. Ian, a large boy, was no sportsman of any kind, but he had a curious interest in making bombs and then taking them to the school grounds and blowing up old petrol drums.

On this particular day, Ian came to our house to make the bomb. We had three rooms outside our house at the back which could be used as accommodation for servants or as workshops. We did not have any permanent servants so we used one of the rooms for a workshop; another was the place to which I was banished when practising the bagpipes.

This is how Ian proceeded on this occasion. He took a piece of pipe about twenty centimetres long, put it in a vice and then hammered one end closed with a hammer. Then he put an explosive powder mixture into the pipe, placed the pipe back in the vice and (can you believe it?) proceeded to gently hammer the remaining open end of the pipe closed!

All this going on in a back room with my mother inside our house, oblivious to what was going on only metres from her!

Ian then took this bomb plus some fuse wire and we all traipsed to the section of the school ground furthest away from the school building. Ian found an old drum. He placed the bomb under the drum and laid the fuse from the drum to a point a few metres away. When all was ready, he lit the fuse and then we all scampered to safety. The blast was strong enough to lift the drum a few metres off the ground and loud enough to draw attention of passers-by. Fortunately, there were no injuries.

I can add a sad footnote to this story. Years later, after I had left the town, I heard that another friend of ours had sustained serious injuries trying a similar trick with explosives. Luckily, it was not fatal.

Violence was part of society in South Africa at that time, and today even more so. Violence around the possession and use of firearms exacerbates the problem. When we moved to Boksburg from Mafeking in 1950, we were moving to a heavily populated part of the country around Johannesburg where gold was discovered in the 1850s. There was also a huge black and white population with occasionally outbreaks of violence. Robbery was common which was not surprising as the whites had the comfortable homes and wealth, and the blacks lived in shacks on the outskirts of the cities, often without running water or electricity as I pointed out earlier.

My father must have felt some insecurity because he acquired a small pistol ('handgun' as the Americans would say) for protection. To do this, he had to arrange to see the local magistrate and seek permission to buy one. He kept this pistol above his cupboard in his bedroom, and it could only be used with his permission. I never ever saw him actually ever fire the pistol. Nor did we ever use it for protection.

We boys liked to use it in the backyard for occasional shooting practice. Not that we did that often. My eldest brother was occasionally allowed to take it down and then my older brother and I were allowed a shot or two in the backyard.

Although my father did not take to firearms (probably disliked them, as he was a non-violent person), I discovered that I had a good eye for shooting. It happened like this. At high school, we had what was called 'cadets'. That is, we had to dress in khaki uniform on one day a week and were then taught how to march ('square bashing') and how to march with rifles and how to present arms (a bit like Parramatta Volunteer Rifles, which Frederick Armitage introduced at King's School Parramatta, Sydney in 1859[19]). We were a small army as the whole high school were cadets. I did not mind this bit of exercise. I was so good at it that they made me a sergeant! The marching was all done on a public road near the school.

Let me add a note. Later in my teaching career, after I graduated from university, I qualified as a 'commissioned officer' precisely because I had a university degree. I was never given any training or induction to being a commissioned officer. They simple gave me all the uniforms and paraphernalia that went with it, without any explanation as to when and how it was to be used. I always felt very uncomfortable in this uniform with hat, gloves and baton.

Back to my story. Because I was now in cadets at high school, the teacher who looked after bisley shooting (competitive rifle shooting) ran a program to discover any talent there might be in the school. The new first-year high school class was tested every year. After one session, if you showed a skerrick of talent, you would be invited to a second trial.

The first sessions were horrific and dangerous, a bit like the Wild West. There were about thirty of us at the shooting range after school. Only four or five lay down at a time to shoot. The rifles were on the ground waiting for the shooters. The teacher had to control every moment of the exercise as some of the boys had little bodily co-ordination and less common sense. Each cadet lay down and looked into a short brick tunnel and then about 20 metres down to the wall in front of which were the decimal targets. However, learning to get a hold of the rifle and rifle strap, and lie down was not easy, especially when the barrel could point in all directions, to the consternation of the teacher and other cadets.

*Bisley team of CBC Boksburg, c.1954.
Author, second row extreme right.*

Author with bisley trophies.

Author in Hunting Stuart uniform, c.1953.

Then the more dangerous task of giving out bullets and showing how to load one. After permission was given to fire one, all eyes were on the targets. Some novices ended up firing at the side of the tunnel wall on the way to the target, others missed the targets and struck the wall behind the targets. I recall one or two bullets ended up ricocheting over our heads. I never figured out how this was even possible.

In no time at all, I was part of the team and continued to practise target shooting at the school. At the age of twelve, I was part of the team that went to Wemmer Pan (an old, disused goldmine dump) for the Johannesburg schools' annual bisley. There were three age divisions, sub-junior, junior and senior. I was in the sub-junior group. I did not think I was the best in the junior group from our school but, as I recall, that discussion just never came up.

We fired ten deliberative rounds (bullets) and ten rapid rounds. Like many others, I preferred the rapid fire because you did not have the time to repeat taking aim before you fired. With deliberative fire, you have too much time to wonder if you should pull the trigger or take aim again. As the bullets were fired into the mine dump, you could hear the echo of many shots in the crevices in the dump. If any cadet fired after the whistle had gone to stop firing, there was a dramatic inquisition as to 'who fired that shot?'

When all the cadets had finished, we milled around waiting for the results. Our teacher came up to me with a rather startled look on his face, and said I had won the sub-junior event with a 94/100 score, and quickly gave me a coaching lesson on how to march up, salute and accept my trophy from the big chief, step back, salute again and then disappear. When I got home, my mother was likewise surprised when I pitched up at the front door with this huge trophy.

My father said little at first about my achievement, but sometime in the next few days, he said he wanted to take a photo of me with my trophies. There was the very large *Floating Trophy* which had to be handed back after a number of months, and the small one you could keep forever as a souvenir. My father was very proud of me but was never verbose in his feelings. I have this photo to this day.

Now that I write this story, one aspect I had never thought of before comes to mind. To my best recollection, the school never made any mention of this at their assemblies. Today, seventy years later, I notice how positive and rewarding school assemblies are. I think this shows a huge and progressive change in school culture. We did have assemblies, of course, but the main point was usually complaints about the pupils misbehaving at the local railway stations or at the Café on the way to school. That I never expected the assemblies to mention my success (and so never missed it) is perhaps a poor reflection of the school culture at that time in history – or perhaps that rugby and athletics were the major sports, and bisleys were a mere footnote.

My hobbies were mainly sports, like rugby, tennis soccer and fretwork which I learnt from a friend. Although I never pursued shooting as a hobby or sport as I grew up, I did acquired a love for classical music which got stronger with age. This might partly have been influenced by my father who liked to sit in the lounge in the dark and listen to classical music.

For another lucky escape I need to fast forward many years to our wedding day. My future wife, Caroline, whom

I met on a tennis court in Rome, and, like me, was working at the Food and Agriculture Organisation (FAO) in Rome, had fixed the date of our wedding for 2 June in the pretty baroque church of Sant'Anna in the Vatican City. Actually Sant'Anna is the parish church of the Vatican. If you walk along via Borgo Pio towards the Vatican with your back to the Tiber, you can cross over the via di Porta Angelica and through the gates with Swiss guards on duty, and then immediately to your right is the church.

All the arrangements had been organised by Caroline and everything went off perfectly. At least, that is what I thought. Being a Friday, we had decided to go travelling in Umbria for the weekend because we had to go back to work on the Monday. Booking seemed unnecessary on this weekend. So after the wonderful wedding service and reception, we headed off to Umbria only to find that in Todi all the *pensioni* (hotels) were booked out, being the national convention of the Christian Democrat Party.

So we travelled on after dark to find that the neighbouring Perugia was also booked out. Plunging further into the night and darkness we finally entered Gubbio (of Francis of Assisi fame) and after many inquires a couple said their friend had accommodation for us for the night. I did not earn any brownie points for that miscalculation.

However, the story had a positive side to it. On the actual wedding day, the Friday, the Italian Airforce gave us a flypast with the plumes of white, red and green smoke for the Italian flag. It was of the *Festa Della Repubblica*, the Italian National Day, 2 June!

There is another lucky escape which comes to mind unrelated to the above. This was a financial lucky escape. Once I had turned sixty, I began to think about retiring. I was totally against the idea of working until one drops dead with exhaustion. My idea was to spend some time with my grandchildren, if, and when, they arrived. However, with regard to the timing of retirement, the challenge is to work out if your pension is enough to live on.

After much cogitation and input from the super fund, I decided that 2006 was a good year to retire. This I did and two years later the Global Financial Crisis hit all and sundry. A number of my colleagues had planned to retire in 2008 but suddenly found out that their savings were significantly diminished. This meant they had to continue working for a few more years to make up the loss, due to the GFC. I considered myself very lucky to have escaped this crisis given that I had no knowledge of the impending financial catastrophe.

In spite of the crises I lived through, there were many moments of wonderment and fascination with planet Earth while travelling the globe. I will turn to some of these occasions now.

7

Travelling this beautiful planet

Travel has many pleasant and interesting memories for me. Sometimes events were amusing, sometimes exhausting, but always fascinating. That I was able to travel was very fortunate. The time was after WWII and so relative peace prevailed. There was also no great global pandemic until the corona virus appeared in 2020. For the period of relative peace I am eternally grateful.

Travelling has its ups and downs. I think of the time in northern Italy when I was driving a hired car for sightseeing. I was stopped by a dapper policeman on a small mountain road, who politely asked to see my driving licence. This I duly produced, having purchased an international driving licence some years prior to this visit to Italy. He carefully examined and read this licence turning over the pages with great interest. This might have been his first look at an international licence. I don't think he could read much as there were a number of languages used in the licence. Finally, he returned the licence to me with a broad smile of gratitude having been given a new experience. I was greatly relieved because he had failed to read the cover page which clearly showed the licence was out of date!

Another memorable trip was on the train returning to Italy after spending some summertime in Bonn learning German. I had tried to renew my sojourn document (for Italy) while in Bonn in what was then West Germany, but was told at the Italian embassy in Bonn to come back when

I was closer to my departure date. I did not see the point in this reply as I was travelling in a week's time, but what could I do? I failed to return as the embassy was rather off the beaten track.

Consequentially, I boarded the train which went via Munich to Innsbruck in Austria, then down through the breathtaking landscape to the beautiful Brenner Pass and into Italy. From the Brenner Pass, I travelled through Bolzano to Verona and thence on to Rome. But I am getting ahead of my story.

At the Brenner Pass border, a security guard boarded the train checking passports or sojourn documents (like the gestapo in a WWII movie). Having read my documents, he told me to get off the train while other passengers looked at me as if I was a terrorist and were thankful that I had been out-ed.

The guard took me to the station master's office where I had to do some explaining to the station master. I told him in halting Italian I too was surprised that my documents were out of date and that I was merely a humble student studying in Rome. I looked as remorseful as I could summons up. He heard me out then he told me get back on the train and get the documents updated in Rome. I gratefully retreated onto the waiting train which I had delayed. I realise now, post 9/11, that I might have received far harsher treatment if this had happened today.

My fellow students in Europe thought I was being rather risky when we visited West Berlin in 1969. (After WWII, Germany was divided into two – West Germany and the DDR, the Deutsche Demokratische Republik, and so was its capital, Berlin.) In order to get to Berlin one had to travel on the highway through the DDR into Berlin which was divided into various sectors. In the west were the British, American and French zones (known as West Berlin), and then, in the east was East Berlin which was communist and part of the DDR.

People were not allowed to go into East Berlin unless they had the okay from the Communists. So we drove into the DDR at the border town of Helmstedt (West Germany), and then were told by the Communist border guards to keep doing 100km/h and not to stop!! We certainly did this, not wanting to get on the wrong side of soldiers with automatic rifles at the ready.

Once inside West Berlin, we were keen to see East Berlin for which we had to go through Check Point Charlie. On approaching this border check, we were confronted by guards with machineguns. They made us get out of the car and then searched under the car with mirrors stuck onto long poles. The car had then to zig-zag its way through the chicanes (checkpoint barriers) – this was to prevent anyone from the East escaping to the West by charging through at high speed. In spite of the barrier poles being fairly low, some individuals did get through by using a low sports car, deflating the tyres, and then racing through.

Once through the checkpoint, we walked around admiring the Brandenburg Gate and the soldiers who guarded some important buildings. I was adventurous enough to walk up the steps and stand next to the stone-faced guards for a photo which my fellow student took. Many things struck me in East Berlin, especially the drabness and sameness of the streets and apartment blocks with the DDR flag on display from all the apartments.

In August 1968, I was in Germany when the Soviets marched into Czechoslovakia (a communist country at the time) to 'restore order' because of the Prague Spring. The Czechoslovakia leader, Alexander Dubcek had tried in introduce 'socialism with a human face' but soviet leaders feared he was becoming more westernised. What surprised me was the palpable fear and angst among Germans that this invasion might extend further west, thus bringing back bad memories of WWII.

Via Rasella, Rome

While in Rome, I often used to go walking on the weekends, searching for some building, palace or site of some historical interest. The bomb explosion in Via Rasella always appalled me. Via Rasella is pretty much in the centre of Rome which at the time of this incident, was under German control. On 23 March 1944, the German police regiment of 156 men was returning to its barracks (a large palazzo) in Via Rasella, when a bomb that the Italian *Gruppi di Azione Patriottica* (Patriotic Action Group) – an Italian partisan group of 17 partisans) – had planted for them, was detonated. Thirty-two Germans soldiers were killed, 110 wounded, and two civilian bystanders.

In a reprisal, the Germans took 10 Italians for every German killed and transported them to the outskirts of Rome to the 'fosse Ardeatine' – caves that were actually the remnants of Christian catacombs. Under the direction of Nazi General Jodl, they shot the lot of them which was 335 in total – a number larger than it should have been. The incident is now honoured by a memorial in the cave itself which attracts many tourists.

It is these acts of utter cruelty and desperation that makes one consider the evil of war and hatred. The pointlessness of war is something that many of us discover sooner or later. I often think of the WWI and the slaughter that went on in the trenches in Europe, or the futility of the ANZAC attempts in 1915/1916, to storm the heights in Gallipoli Peninsula, or indeed of the acceptance of losing 60% of the soldiers who stormed the French beaches on 6 June 1944. There are many such historical cases.

More recently, one thinks of the recurring loss of life in battles in and over Afghanistan, the Ukraine or Palestine. My response is always: I cannot stop such carnage but I can promote kindness and support to those near to me. We often glorify war (some protest saying we are only 'honouring the dead') rather than build memorials to peace.

Similar thoughts went through my head when I visited Monte Casino monastery in southern Italy, 139 km southeast of Rome. It is here that some of the fiercest fighting of the Italian campaign took place in 1943-4. On the hilltop where the monastery is located you can look down on the cemetery where 4271 soldiers lie buried – all victims of WWII. The beautifully kept cemetery is a constant reminder of the futility of war. Looking down over the cemetery, I was moved yet once again to lament the aphorism that there are no winners in war.

The problem with Italy is that there are too many special places that need to be visited! The sites of interest in Italy are from the period of BCE, the rise and growth of Christianity, and then two World Wars. There is too much to be seen. In this respect, it is like Palestine and Israel where there are so many layers of history to explore.

Author and wife at New Grange, Ireland, 2000

Anyway, back to Italy: I recall one temple site which people often overlook, and that is *Paestum* near Naples. It dates from the period 550-450 BCE. Actually, Paestum was a Greek city near the Tyrrhenian coast, but today only the well-preserved remains of the three Doric temples are to be seen. Largely forgotten in most of the second millennium, they were rediscovered in the eighteenth century.

Thinking about the war era recalls to mind our visit to Taizé in Burgundy, France. In August 2001, Caroline and I did a car trip from Geneva airport to Taizé, a small French village, which is near Macon and Cluny. The Taizé ecumenical community was started, after WWII, by Brother Roger Schutz, son of a Lutheran pastor, who would not accept the way Christian churches had accepted division and hatred among denominations (like my father). He thought it absolutely hypocritical the way some profess to be Christian but treated fellow Christians in an abominable way. His movement grew and was especially supported by the young.

Seize the day

Caroline at San Gimignano, Italy

Caroline and I lodged in nearby Cluny, in the *Hotel Saint Odilon*, run by a welcoming *Monsieur et Madame* Robert Berry. It was what we would call and B&B, but did offer a tasty *petit déjeuner* after which we would spent the day at Taizé, witnessing the way young people would spend time in the church in silent prayer and how they celebrated lunch with visitors, picnic-style out in the open.

There is much I could say about France and its beauty. Its attractions are annually projected to the world on TV with the world-famous *Tour de France* cycling race. Earlier on in my life, as a student, I had the privilege of studying French at Tour (I knew nothing to begin with, and not much more at the end!) and was taken by the local family with whom I was staying to visit the unforgettable and remarkable chateaux of the rich in the Loire valley, like Chenonceau, Chambord, Amboise, Blois and the abbey of Fontevraud which, although for men and women (in different parts of the monastery), was run by an abbess! Not bad for a church usually known for its misogyny!

While talking about France, I think of another part of the world, namely New Orleans (USA) because of its links to France. I was attending a conference but Caroline was able to accompany me and see some of the city.

This city was of great interest to us. A visit to the mighty Mississippi was one of the first items to see. What impressed me was the height of the levees that had been built to keep out the river. Currently, the river is higher than the city so that any flooding immediately impacts on the city.

The graves in the cemeteries are virtually all above ground to protect them from the high water table. It was explained to us that the majority of New Orleans is built upon reclaimed swampland and much of the city is below sea level. I went to sleep that night thinking about sleeping below sea level! The French influence in New Orleans since the beginning of the 18th century is today still reflected in its impressive architecture and in its French-infused cuisine.

But what is also clear is the capacity of the locals to sing and dance although life for many is very challenging. I can think of one unforgettable incident. Caroline and I were attending a conference dinner in New Orleans when the jazz band started playing. At one stage, the dancers started the conga line dance. In this dance the dancers form a long, processing line which usually turns into a circle. People attending the dinner simply get up from their tables and join the line. But to our surprise, the local waiters and waitresses with obvious enthusiasm, were so turned on by the music that they too joined in the conga line although they were technically on duty. I do not think this would have happened elsewhere in the world. This experience of its rich Afro-American culture is a gift to the world.

Another place of great interest to me and Caroline was the island of Malta in the Mediterranean Sea, which the British held onto during WWII because of its strategic value to North Africa and the Mediterranean arena. Caroline's grandfather was born on the Island. In 2018, we took off from Rome and flew to Malta, a very Christian and small island and now a member of the European Union.

The British culture is still evident and most locals speak fluent English as well as their native Maltese. We were delighted to attend a production of Christopher Marlowe's play, *The Jew of Malta*, while we were there. We also met a woman shop assistant who had lived many years in Australia and now had returned to Malta. Given the large Maltese population of Australia, we were not surprised.

There are many places of interest to visit on Malta. Among these is St Paul's Cave at Rabat, a small town west of Valetta, the capital of Malta, These caves are now cared for by *Heritage Malta*. Paul, the peripatetic Christian apostle, was wrecked there for three months in 60 CE on his way from Cyprus to Rome.

Actually, the way we found our way there was unusual. From Valetta we took a guided tour to Rabat and other sites as a day trip, only to be told belatedly on the bus that we would not be visiting St Paul's cave as the trip had been curtailed. We would be visiting Rabat though.

I was most annoyed by this turn of events, so I decided we would leave the tour at Rabat and catch a taxi for a short trip to the caves. It turned out the taxi driver did not know exactly where these caves were but we eventually found them with some local help. They are hardly spectacular as caves go, but it was impressive to see where Paul had been many years before. After climbing through them, we got back to the spot where we left the bus.

While in Malta, we also made use of our time to visit – by bus then ferry –the extraordinary Megalithic temples on the island of Gozo, which are among the world's oldest free-standing structures, being built between 3600 – 2500 BCE. Some of these temples are now *UNESCO World Heritage* sites. My only complaint was after a long, interrupted bus ride and tedious wait for the ferry, when we finally got to the sights we were told you only have seven minutes to have a look and take photos!

Malta also has a dark side. It is often referred to as 'the Mafia island'. There is the infamous story of a fifty-three year old woman, author and journalist, Daphne Caruana Galizia, murdered there in 2017, just a year before Caroline and I landed in sunny Valetta. At that stage the tragic story had been aired many times in the newspapers but, although no arrests had been made, suspicion was on the politicians who were known for their secrecy, lack of integrity and misogynistic attitudes. Daphne Galizia was subjected to many threats and intimidations by police and others. Finally, a bomb which had been concealed under her car seat, was detonated just a hundred metres from her house.

The reason she was targeted was that she was on to something. The local energy suppler was about to be handed over to one person, Yorgen Fenech, the owner of a Dubai based, 17 Black company. It was suspected that bribes had been paid to the Prime Minister's chief of staff and a minister. When Fenech was arrested, he confessed and the hit men brothers were arrested and eventually sentenced to forty years each in prison.[20] The Prime Minister, Joseph Muscat, has not been charged with anything yet (2022), but resigned as PM.

The vicious death of Daphne Galizia provoked the rise of a feminist movement which was determined to get rid of the corrupt government and politicians for the good and future of their country. The consequences of this sad tale of corruption are still to be fully played out.

Perhaps the most impressive place I visited was the Galapagos Islands, suggested by Caroline when I retired. It is difficult to choose the most impressive or best place, because each place is different and has different charms. I like the Galapagos Islands because they took me back into pre-history and you felt that you were privileged to see things from another era altogether. The islands are often bleak, naked rock promontories with little or no green vegetation.

*Author and Caroline at The Post Office,
on the island of Floreana, Galapagos Islands, 2006.*

We were on a boat large enough to carry about twenty people. Each cabin had two beds. The trip took us around the southern part of the Galapagos over a week. While we slept at night, the boat would sail towards the next island which greeted us in the morning. With each island, those who wanted to go ashore would get into a dingy and be taken there for a few hours. On one occasion, I recall getting out of our little rubber dingy and wading through water onto the island. Everything seemed quiet and eerie, and nothing moved. You only saw the black rocks ahead of you. The island appeared lifeless at first. And then suddenly you took a second look and saw all the sea dragons on the rocks, lying dead still, looking at you and occasionally spitting out salt.

The other lasting memory is that of swimming with the sea lions at another island. We were swimming in fairly shallow waters near the beach but so were the sea lions. They seemed to enjoy our company and would swim past us and give us a gentle nudge as they passed as if to say: 'Welcome, nice to see you!' Any apprehension of the sea lions we had soon turned into joy.

We also witnessed a football/soccer game on one of the islands, between our crew and another belonging to a second tour. We had been carefully told to keep off the natural flora on the island – not to throw our towels on the native bushes, for example, when going for a swim. However, once the game started, these rules of respect for the local flora seemed no longer to apply!

Istanbul is another place I recall with great pleasure. After reading so much about Constantinople (Istanbul) in history, the early Christian Church, the Christian Councils and Emperors, the crusades, the Seljuk and Ottoman Empires, it was a great privilege to finally land there with Caroline in 2014. Our accommodation was in the old city, only a stone's throw away from the Gulhane Park and Topkapi Palace Museum. Close by too was the world famous and stunning Hagia Sofia and the neighbouring Blue Mosque which we visited after the Hagia Sophia and for which tourist women had to wear a veil.

The size and beauty of the Hagia Sophia is something to behold – the word 'transcendence' comes to mind. The murals, many of which have been saved after centuries, are likewise imposing. The history and purpose of this architectural creation has changed over the years, from firstly a Christian Byzantine basilica, then a mosque, then museum and now a mosque again. Thank God it has not been destroyed like the Bamiyan Buddha statues by the Taliban in Afghanistan in 2001.

Not surprisingly, our hotel hosts in Istanbul had difficulty knowing what we were talking about when we enquired about the whereabouts of the palace of the Ecumenical Patriarch in Fener. After a diversion, we found the cathedral of St George which is next to the Palace. While walking across to the Palace, we totally unexpectedly came across an Orthodox pastor and friend we knew from Sydney, John Chryssavgis, who kindly gave us a guided tour of the palace.

From l. to r: John Chryssavgis, Caroline and author, at the palace of the Ecumenical Patriarch, Fener, Istanbul, 2004.

After visiting St George's cathedral, not finding a taxi, we walked to a smaller church called Chora Church (Church of the Holy Saviour in Chora) which has some of the oldest surviving Byzantine Christian mosaics and frescoes. Again, this was a privilege to visit.

President Erdogan has tried to turn this building into a mosque but in 2021 the reversion was stopped due to a lack of Islamic cultural significance! After doing all this in one morning and somewhat exhausted with all the walking, we finally found a taxi at the Chora Church, who overcharged us on the return journey to our hotel. Nevertheless, he might have needed the money more than we did.

Another city which I had the privilege of visiting was Jerusalem. Again as with Istanbul, Jerusalem is a city about which I had heard and read so much. It was a tremendous emotional experience to actually jump on a plane in Rome and fly to Jerusalem. It was the time of great tension in Israel (is it not always that way?) with the Japanese Red Army, recruited by the Palestinian group called the Popular Front for the Liberation of Palestine, having attacked Lod airport on 30 May 1972 and killed 26 people (known as the Lod Airport massacre).

At Lod airport (more recently changed to Ben Gurion Airport), when our plane pulled up on the tarmac, we were told to remain sitting in our seats, holding our passports in our raised hands. Security came on board and worked their way down the aisle. At a certain point they dragged two men out of the plane and took them behind a nearby truck (I could see out of my plane window what was going on). They frisked them and then took them off somewhere. Whew! What an introduction to a new country!! Not exactly a relaxed arrival!

Caroline and I were on a FAO (Food and Agricultural Organisation) organised tour of The Holy Land, so we moved around a lot and were introduced to so many historical sites, both BCE and CE, that after a while, we felt our brains becoming tired trying to take it all in. Our guide, Moshe, was just terrific with his incredible depth of knowledge of local history. Something I will never forget was dancing at the hotel in Tiberius on the Sea of Galilee with the sound of shelling in the distance on the Golan Heights (the Israeli army was shelling Syrian positions).

Given our scary introduction to Israel, our exit was a bit frightening too. I had asked our trusty Israeli bus driver to stop somewhere where I could buy a couple of bottles of Israeli wines to take back to Rome. As the tour would last 11 days, there was no hurry to purchase the wines. However, in the end, the bus driver had failed to stop anywhere for the wine, but when we got to the airport to leave he gave me three bottles of white wine.

Passing through security, they asked me if I had any presents and I unthinkingly said 'no'. Then they asked me what was in my plastic bad and I said two bottles of wine. He opened the bag to find three bottles! Where did I get them? Well, the bus driver gave them to me. My story was not looking good at this stage, so they shunted me off to a cubicle where they could frisk me and examine the wines. He held the bottles up to the light to carefully examine their contents. He seemed happy with the result and as he found nothing untoward, he returned them to me.

On this trip, we also decided to take a gift back to our friends in Switzerland whom we planned to visit. We chose lovely wholesome avocados, thinking this would be a great surprise and speciality for our friends. When we eventually got to Switzerland, the expression on their faces on receiving the gift, left us aghast. They had never seen avocados before and would not eat them! Beware Greeks bearing gifts!

Another place and experience which left an indelible impression on Caroline and me was the eleventh century

St Mark's Basilica in Venice with its touches of Byzantine, Romanesque and Islamic elements. A highpoint here was attendance at Sunday liturgy in the cathedral.

On Sundays, the basilica's main entrance was closed to tourists and those who wanted to attend the Eucharistic celebration had to enter via a side door. Whether you were a 'tourist' or 'worshipper' was up to you to decide. I know of one 'worshipper' who entered with us and was sitting near us, suddenly got up and exited after viewing the mosaics! For me as a Christian, it was a great privilege to be sitting in this ancient basilica of Christianity admiring all the golden mosaics decorating the vaults and walls. Most of them depicted a biblical theme. Now to do this while listening to the beautiful singing of a visiting German choir was a definite highpoint for me. At this moment, I agreed with the poet, John Keats, when he proclaimed, 'a thing of beauty is a joy forever'. While enjoying these sights and sounds, I was able to surreptitiously take a photo of a floor mosaic of a peacock (a symbol of eternity) right next to me.

A mosaic of a Peacock, about 800 years old, a symbol of Eternity, on the floor of the Basilica di San Marco, Venice.

Switching to the other side of the globe is the sacred valley of the Incas, also worthy of a visit. We visited this in 2006 after we had been to the Galapagos Islands. We saw, first-hand, Machu Picchu, the mysterious 15th century Inca citadel perched on top of the Andes northwest of Cusco in Peru.

This put us in touch with a past group of scholars who studied the stars and mountains from their mountaintop view. They would have known of the wheel because they used logs to roll things around on the mountain top. Build with solid dry stone walls, it has weathered the centuries. For many centuries, it was hidden and forgotten until the 19th century. Again, for me, the feeling of touching something of a cultural value from our collective human past, a World Heritage site, was indeed overwhelming.

To get to Machu Picchu we chose the train trip from Cusco well aware that many younger people take one of the many mountain tracks to reach it. The train takes a zigzag track up the hillside to get out of Cusco. As the train slowly works its way up the gradient, it passes by, at very close range, the many poor and squalid houses beside the track. That image still lingers on in my memory. On the day and in the train, one's view changes as you get into the mountains with the impressive view looking up through the glass roof of the carriage. When the train reaches *Agua Calientes*, you have a 6 km road trip by bus to get to the actual *Manchu Picchu* location.

Author and Caroline at Machu Picchu, 2006.

This sense of heritage and cultural value is something our generation needs to ponder. The recent destruction of Yakuun Caves in Western Australia, and other destruction of cultural icons, makes me think that money has become our God and we no longer value cultural heritage. I hope First Nation peoples can bring us to our senses.

Having often seen the White House on the TV screen, I never thought I would one day be inside it. This is how it happened. I was on sabbatical which included a period at the Catholic University of America in Washington. D.C. I have two cousins in the States and one of them told me his wife had a brother who worked at the White House as a security person. He was able to get me a ticket for a guided visit to the White House.

And so, on a given morning, I met my contact in a café near the White House for a bagel and coffee before I started my visit. I was struck by the size of the place. It was not at all as large as the spacious palaces one sees in Europe for heads of state. Nevertheless we were shown around, including the Eastern Wing where the press conferences take place. There was no sign of the president, of course, but I appreciated the opportunity to visit the home of the US president.

I have had the privilege of travelling by car, train and plane, but not yet by spaceship! From childhood, I have favoured the train as a mode of travel perhaps because one can move around on the train and not be confined to one seat. The train trip that I cherish most was that which I did in August 2001, from Graz in Austria through Innsbruck and Zurich and finally arriving in Lausanne in Switzerland in one day.

I had been attending a work conference in Graz and Caroline was visiting a friend in Switzerland so I decided to go to Lausanne by train. It was a truly unforgettable day. Ensconced in my window seat, I watched the incredibly beautiful mountainous scenery as we glided from one glorious idyllic valley to the next with all the chalets showing off their flowerbox geraniums (red, pink and white) and the meadows covered with a variety of arnicas, bellflowers, primulas, white poppies and even orchids.

These are all truly wonderful experiences etched in my consciousness. One thing that sticks in my mind is how similar people are throughout the world. We may have different languages and customs but we are one humankind. That unity aspect has often come under attack when religions interact as we shall see below.

8

Walking together

One Bread, One Body

The issue of a divided Christianity and how to bring the churches together (ecumenism) is one which has demanded my attention for many years. As I pointed out in an earlier chapter, my younger sister has noted that I seem to follow in the path of my father with regard to ecumenism.

Growing up, I had noted that my father was trying to persuade Afrikaans-speaking people that the Catholics were not as bad as they thought. He was all for building bridges between the two groups. As already mentioned, he wrote articles for a magazine called *Die Brug* (The Bridge) which was a Catholic magazine in Afrikaans (unusual for those times). He was appalled by the constant vitriolic letter writing that went on in the papers against the 'Roomse gevaar' (Roman danger). How can people behave like that if both groups call themselves Christians?

The context in which I grew up was the sectarianism of the 20th century whereby Christian churches often attacked each other in a very unchristian way. That had been the case since the Reformation in the sixteenth century. The bad feelings manifested themselves in different ways in different countries. In Germany, it was Lutherans and Catholics; in France, Calvinists and Catholics; in Scotland, Presbyterians and Catholics; in South Africa, the Dutch Reform Church and the Catholics. In some cases, it was Catholics against any Protestant church. In Northern Ireland, the Catholic and the Protestant feud is well known throughout the western world.

The founding of the World Council of Churches in 1948 did much to address the scandalous situation among Christians, but for Catholics they had to wait until the Second Vatican Council (1962-65) to address this issue seriously. Over the next fifty years, the churches began respecting each other and producing some really progressive documents in which they explored common ground and beliefs.

It was only when I was able to teach courses in ecumenism at university level that I was able to study the conceptual side of the disagreement, while simultaneously working with interchurch groups at the local level to see what could be done collaboratively. I quickly discovered that some Catholic bishops were either lukewarm or anti-ecumenism, while a few were really passionate about it, like Bede Heather, bishop of Parramatta diocese in Australia, in the 1980s. A strong conviction I have is that too many bishops set up Ecumenism Commissions because Rome told them to, but made sure they were pretty anodyne.

On the other hand, many ordinary folk at the local level were totally for the churches to come together. I recall when we had our first local ecumenical event which was a cake stall and banner which read 'Churches Working Together'. An elderly lady came up to the stall and read the banner and then drily commented, 'About time!'

There were many reasons why the clergy and laity saw the ecumenical movement differently. Let me give one insight. Those clergy who see their church as having all the truth are reluctant to make any move that might legitimise another church, while a lay person in a 'mixed' marriage (each spouse from a different church) might still be suffering from the way their church treated them at the time of their marriage. They would see better relationships between churches as avoiding the bitterness they experienced.

I would like to make a comment on the assumption some people have – that their church has all the truth. At the heart of this problem is the assumption that truth can only be expressed one way. This is false. The actual truth is one thing, the manner in which it is expressed is another. The truth is often so profound that it cannot be adequately expressed in only one way.

The negative attitude of churches towards each other is succinctly stated by the former assistant bishop in Sydney, Geoffrey Robinson, when he states that all he ever heard about other Christian churches from his lecturer Piolanti in Rome in the 1960s was under the heading of 'Errors'.[21] By the way, Piolanti, who was ultra conservative, became *Rector Magnificus* (Vice Chancellor) of the Lateran University where I studied.

Because Italy is overwhelmingly nominally Catholic, Italians in general never got to know members of other churches, so they were very surprised and curious when I told them I knew many Protestant Christians. They wanted to know what they were like. What did I think of them?

There is an issue in ecumenism – in the background – that needs to be discussed. If two churches are progressing so well in discussions that unity seems possible, there is the threat for bishops involved – of who will be the bishop if they unite? No king likes to lose his kingdom. I sense that this might be one issue preventing the union of the Assyrian Church of the East and Chaldean Catholic Church, in spite of their *Common Christological Declaration* in 1994. A colleague of mine in the ecumenical council remarked quite astutely that whenever two churches got close in their movement towards unity, one or other would raise the bar to keep unity at bay.

My work for the New South Wales Ecumenical Council in the 1980s and 1990s was also an opportunity to experience how other churches work and contribute in a variety of ways to promote better understandings among churches.

One of the most fruitful connections and experiences I had was the Refugee program in NSW. The federal government had a program in place whereby a group of people, a parish group for example, could come together and agree to help settle a refugee family over a period of six months. A limited amount of money came from the government to get the family started with rentals, food, etc.

So we (lay people) from our already established interchurch group formed a committee of representatives from the various churches and approached the co-ordinating woman, Jenny Johnson, of the NSW Ecumenical Council, and said we would like to settle a family.

Jenny heard me out and then said that it was a big undertaking and we should give some more thought to it. In time, we did give it more thought. I offered to visit all the pastors of the various churches involved to get their support as I knew that we would probably do some fund raising at some stage. I knew pastor consultation would be easy with some and a challenge with others who had reservations.

One pastor in particular responded to my invitation thus: 'Gideon, I presume we will get a Christian family to settle'. I had to admit I did not know. I knew many were coming from Iraq and many Iraqis were Muslims. So we went ahead and applied to settle a family.

The system was that the NSW Ecumenical Council told the government that we had a group ready to settle a family. We were told to be on standby since they did not know when the next family would arrive.

In due course, we were told a family was on the way, so we jumped into action looking for a suitable home for rental. Our team, under the coaching of Jenny, had divided up the tasks among the committee members. Members took on one of the many aspects of settlement: finding out about schools and helping them approach the school; helping with the banking system; understanding Centrelink; helping with transport and shopping; knowing all about the health system.

We were fortunate to find a house pretty close to everything in Glenbrook, NSW. I was told the family was Muslim but I thought it prudent not to pass on this information. It would be a family of two children, a father and a pregnant mother. On the night that we had to meet them at the airport, we set off in our cars and seem to wait an eternity before they were visible at the end of a long stream of passengers. Communications was a problem. Fortunately for us, we had a native speaker with us who helped out.

I will never forget the night. It was cold and misty with light rain here and there. The family travelled in a fleet of cars for more than an hour to get to Glenbrook. I often wondered what thoughts were going through the minds of the mother and father and children. Did they find this a strange place, with people who spoke a different language? Did they wonder where they would sleep on their first night in Australia, and what would the tomorrow bring? I think they were pleasantly surprised to arrive at the house and see how comfortable it had been made for them, down to details like soft toys for the children.

The response of the local people was overwhelming in its generosity. We did have a few requests for donations for furniture before they arrived. One person took out his cheque book and wrote me a cheque for $100 on the spot. He said his parents were refugees from Poland many years prior to that and they had received help when they arrived. Now he too wanted to help. Someone else donated a double bed. We had a collection in the old parish church in Glenbrook, St Finbar's (now the hall), and when the parish pastor saw the takings he said: 'Gideon, that is more than I get on a Sunday!'

Before they arrived in Australia, one reservation that a friend of mine had related to employment in Australia. Would they be able to find work? There was always the spurious threat that refugees might be taking Australian jobs away from the locals. I said I did not know. Now I can say the husband did get a job with a dairy company and the children all have jobs now as adults. A second migrant family, I can report, had two sons and two daughters who all went into the catering business and now, some thirty years later, continue to expand and employ young Australians!

I must add this little story about the migrants. We Christians are often very critical about our churches, which in itself is fine, provided we try to be simultaneously constructive in our criticism. Sometime after we had settled a few families, there was a meeting, a celebration of the work the NSW Ecumenical Council has done in settling migrants.

A spokesperson for the migrants who was reasonably fluent in English, addressed the meeting. He spoke about how incredibly impressed he and other migrants were with the 'Christian Churches' which helped him and their families settle in – took them to do shopping, found rental accommodation for them, introduced them to Centrelink, and the banking system, went to local schools with them to place their children.

This was the face of Christianity in Australia that they encountered. What a lovely experience for us to hear that! It just shows you a perspective on churches we might be inclined to overlook or neglect.

Sadly, the Australian government stopped this program for reasons unknown to me. In my experience, it proved positive from so many angles. I must add another instructive incident. The committee which looked after the first family used to meet once a month or so. After a few meetings, one of members blurted: Did we know that the family members were Muslims?' Some said yes, they did, others were mildly surprised. Then someone else commented: 'Well, does it matter?'

And we all agreed that whether you are Muslim, Christian, Buddhist, Hindu, Sikh or Bahá'i, you need education, health care, a job and food. The religion of the refugee family never became a problem among us. This supports my long-held view that if you can get to know the stranger as a person first, other aspects, like their religion, will not be an obstacle to friendship.

I also found contact with the World Council of Churches (WCC) – over some years – to be insightful and instructive. On an earlier study leave, I visited WCC headquarters in Geneva and later while attending a European Society of

Catholic Theologians (ESCT) conference in Fribourg, was part of a trip to Geneva and the WCC.

One of the problems of the Catholic Church is that its systems are medieval and not able to cope with modern ways of doing things. Let me talk from my experience of ecumenism which stands for the change of direction taken by the authorities in the Catholic Church regarding its relationship with other Christian Churches.

The Council of the Catholic Church announced its new direction at Vatican II (1962-5). Although the majority of bishops voted in favour of this change, when they got back to their dioceses some had second thoughts. Rome insisted that each diocese should have a Commission for Ecumenism which meets from time to time and reports back to Rome. Their motivation for doing so could be questioned. Could it be they do it in order to keep in the good books of the Roman authority?

Some pastors – and not only bishops – were (and are) lukewarm about ecumenism. I am not sure why. To some extent, they might have seen the movement as taking their flock away from them, or at least being a distraction from the main game. I can give one example.

A pastor, from another country, working in Australia, was against us (a local interchurch group) going to the Uniting Church for a service like *World Day of Prayer*. He said if some (Catholics) go, they will all become members of the Uniting Church! Another one said he did not want the covenant we had signed with other churches to continue. He gave no reason.

I was convinced he had no knowledge of the document called *Unitatis Redintegratio* (restoration of Unity) of Vatican II which explains it all, although he had done his studies for ordination. It was also the case that the bishop who knew this did not take any action, to my knowledge. Somehow, some bishops are afraid to challenge, or correct, their ministers/pastors. That is another burning issue which needs to be addressed.

I can summarise thus: some pastors are positively against ecumenism and others just do nothing. In some way, it is seen as a threat to their ministry. That might raise the question of what is their ministry. Is it one of 'walking with' or is it one of 'dictating how, when and where you walk'?

I worked at the New South Wales Ecumenical Council for many years in the 1980s-2006, as a member and chair of the Theological Reflection Commission. I came across a report from a well-respected clergyman who stated quite transparently, that, in general, ministers/pastors were the greatest obstacle to ecumenism. There you are! This has been my experience too.

A corollary to this is that Catholics generally will obey their parish pastor. If he says something is good, they will do it. If he is against it, so are they. Because Catholics have done this for centuries, they have an inordinate dependence of their pastor, on authority. This culture is going to be difficult to change.

What is hopeful is that the younger generations can think differently and act independently. If they like the type of service in another church, or a different religion, like Hare Krishnas, they might try it out, whereas the older generation would say Father says 'no' to that group so we must obey. In spite of the above, a small minority of Catholics have had very harsh experiences at the hands of their church, regarding so-called 'mixed' marriages and they can see that antagonism towards other Christian churches is unjust. They are now prepared to work with other churches.

Let me return to the issue raised above about some bishops being reluctant to raise delicate issues with their pastors. Some bishops appear to be afraid that the pastors might leave their assignment and walk away if criticised by them. I think this arises because the pastors have too much power. As Caroline jokingly asks: 'Who would want to be pope if you can be parish priest!' I believe this is true. If pastors had less power, were responsible to a group of laypeople as well as to their bishop, we would have more balance in our governance. (Likewise the bishop's power needs to be re-addressed.) The opportunity at reforming this aspect of governance was available at the time of the Reformation, but the Council of Trent rejected it.

Let me move on to a lighter, but nevertheless telling, incident. I can recall the whole affair with a degree of amusement. I was going to Rome and wrote to the person in charge of the Department for Promoting Christian Unity. This was Kurt Koch, formerly archbishop of Basel, a predominantly German-speaking Swiss city. He had only recently been appointed by Pope Benedict head of that department (called 'dicastery' in Roman terms) and was finding his way.

To my surprise, in our correspondence, he agreed to see me. I and Caroline, after a bus ride from our accommodation in Via Nazionale, Rome, fronted up on the appointed day at the Via della Conciliazione (near St Peter's) and had to search around for the right street number. These palazzos are big and spacious inside. We succeed in finding the right number, and caught the lift upstairs and were taken into a waiting room.

I did not wait long before Koch's secretary came and took me into Koch's office, leaving Caroline in the waiting room. After the usual polite niceties, we searched around for a common language we would use. I said I could speak Italian, but not much French, and my speaking German was not good. He very quickly said English was okay. So off I went and spoke about who I was and what questions I had. After some time, I slowed down and gave him a chance to say something. Well, he started asking me questions about who I was and what work I was doing. Then the penny dropped and I realised he had not understood a word I had said! So much for that!

Later, to many of the questions I put to him, he said he did not know the answer as he was new in the job. One of my questions related to an invitation of John Paul II in *Ut unum sint* where he invites Church leaders and theologians to help him discover how to exercise his ministry more effectively in the light of recent ecumenical developments. His precise words were for 'Church leaders and their theologians to engage with me in a patient and fraternal dialogue on this subject'.[22]

The question was how the pope in Rome could be leader of all Christians, not just Catholics. How could the papacy be exercised in this situation? This was an outreach by way of an invitation from the Pope (through Cardinal Cassidy) to all Christians (including Catholics). We never heard another word about this invitation! And Kurt Koch confessed to me that he was not aware of what had happened to this project.

When I suggested some changes in policy matters like not using the terms 'non-Catholic' or 'non-Christian' in formal documents – as they defined people negatively and made the presumption that 'Catholic' and 'Christian' were the norm – the alternatives could be, 'members of other Christian churches' or 'other faiths', Koch was quick to say the pope will tell us if any changes are needed!

The message was clear: no suggestions are welcome. If there are any changes to be made, the pope will decide. As the quip goes: 'When I want your opinion I will give it to you!' This was all before synodality was invoked. In short, the meeting was not a howling success from my point of view.

The above paragraph mentions members of other faiths. Relationships with Judaism, Islam, Hinduism, etc., had not been a focus for Catholics until the 1960s. In my lifetime, within Catholicism and Christianity in general, there has been a seismic shift from focusing on one's own religion (navel gazing) to focusing on other Christian churches, to other world faiths. The image of expanding concentric circles comes to mind.

When growing up, a child is conscious of itself and its mother, then the circles expands to include other family members, neighbours and pre-school, then local community, etc. But in religion we were inclined to stop at our own religious community and not look over the fence. Now we are strong enough to dare to dialogue with others.

In this sense, I welcome the widening of the horizons of our religious consciousness to include people of all faiths and no religious faith. Or to express it in another way, in my lifetime, the focus of religious consciousness has moved from hatred between Christian churches to tolerance, to interest in other world religions, to embracing the wholehearted inclusiveness of people of all faiths or no faith.

For Catholics, at the official level, this started at Vatican II and perhaps a useful event to highlight this was the visit of Paul VI to Israel in 1964 – the first trip of a pope outside Italy for 500 years, and the first trip ever of a pope to Israel. A second momentous and historic event was Paul VI meeting the Ecumenical Patriarch of Constantinople, Athenagoras I. That marked the first step in a reconciliation process after the Great Schism of 1054, when the Christian church split up into an Eastern (Orthodox) and Western (Catholic) Church. I have a photo of this meeting in my study as a constant reminder of this momentous event.

I see the process of the evolution of the Catholic Church moving further along the road with the election of someone outside Rome and outside Europe, in the election of Jorge Bergoglio as Pope Francis. He is making the Catholic Church a universal church rather than a Roman or European one.

Among other ecumenical developments, this gives me hope for the future. Having discussed various aspects of unity, there remains two very important topics I have left to the last – sexuality and death, the beginning and the end. One cannot complete the journey without reflecting on these.

9

Life without end

My ideas have changed much over the years on all sorts of things. What I wish to do now in this final chapter is to link up a few threads in which there has been significant change. I am thinking of sexuality, marriage, death, resurrection. But before I do this, at the centre of the changes, is the person. It is not the economy, or technology, or society, but the 'person' who is undergoing all this. So it is not a question of trying to join up the beginning and end of life but the way life works its way through many changes, reaching 'omega' point. Let me also add I am convinced we need a language to talk about these issues. A new language that mysticism might help us to explore. That is something to which I aspire.

Who do you think you are?

Let me begin by attempting to describe the idea of a human being or person and then contrast my thinking with the ideas of some neuroscientists. The way one sees human beings is central to the way sees life, and has an obvious connection with thinking about sexuality and death.

There has always been a number of ways of describing the composition of the human being, depending on the discipline one uses.[23] First, when growing up, the idea of person from a theological viewpoint, was a human being with a body and soul. It was part of the Catholic culture of the times. The *soul* was the more important part of a person and it was something we all had to 'save' so that it could 'get into heaven'.

Over many years, my ideas have changed. First, I never did like the dichotomy of body/soul. This is an imposition of Greek thinking and dualism, whereas the Hebrew understanding always saw the person as one, not as consisting of a material body and spiritual soul. There was no binary approach of body and soul. The person was one. The person was seen as one whole entity, not a combination of some material element and some spiritual element.

If asked today what I thought a human being was, I might say that a human being is an entity which has cognition, emotion and awareness. It is capable of seeing things, thinking about them, and taking action. Although it has a material aspect, it also has a spiritual side that accounts for emotions, aspirations and motivation. Each person is unique. At the core of every human being is a unique 'person'. Some humans think the person is annihilated at death; others, like myself, that the person lives on in some way.

More to the point, today I would add that human beings are relational by nature. The human being, to fulfil itself, to develop fully, must relate to four thing: self, others, the material world (environment), and God (a source of all being). All these relationships need teasing out.

In contrast to the above, there is a viewpoint, held by some neuroscientists, that there is only the material aspect of human beings. All other phenomena are the result of the interaction of chemicals in the body. Aspects like feelings, moods, a 'spiritual' dimension, are the result of the interaction of chemicals in the body. There is no objective 'soul', or 'inner self', or 'individual person' just chemicals that interact, producing weird and wonderful results. I cannot accept this understanding of the human being.

I have outlined how I think about the human person but my thinking is also supported by my life's experience. To me, when a child is born, we get to know the child, the person of the child as they develop and grow. The infant at first does not react much to people, but as it grows, we discover, we experience the 'character' of the emerging child. We learn to distinguish the child by its selfhood.

We get to know how the child thinks, what it likes, who it likes, what toys it likes to play with, what its talents are, and how it reacts to mother, father and siblings. Collectively, this points to the depth of the personhood of the child. Thus the experience of getting to know individuals, does not allow me to think of the child as only the result of certain chemical reactions. The determination and the way some of us value this aspect of the self, the inner person, is interesting. Let me jump to an example not often mentioned but striking. It concerns the famous movie fictional figure of James Bond.

Let me refresh our collective memory. Ian Fleming wrote the hugely successful stories about the superman spy, James Bond. The novels became lucrative movies. Of all the Bond actors in the movies, Sean Connery is perhaps the most well-known. But there is one who only played James Bond once, the Australian George Lazenby. The story of how he got the part is most fascinating as he had no previous acting experience.

Only when he followed his then-girlfriend from Sydney to London did someone discover he would make a good male model. He proved to be a very popular one indeed. This led to other things and to the pivotal point when he agreed to apply for the part of James Bond in an upcoming movie called *On Her Majesty's Secret Service*. To his surprise, he got the 007 job without having a past acting career!

Now the part that I find fascinating is that he was successful in this movie and was on the cusp of making millions with future Bond movies. But he rejected the idea saying he wanted to be himself, George Lazenby, not James Bond. What provoked him to take this stance was the attempt of the movie maker at the time to control his life. This entrepreneur wanted Lazenby to be James Bond full-time – even when off the movie set. He instructed him what he was to wear and what he was to attend – always as James Bond. His whole life would be consumed by uninterruptedly pretending to be James Bond.

Fortunately for Lazenby, although he had finished filming *On Her Majesty's Secret Service*, he had not yet signed any contract. So he simply refused to sign and walked away from making millions. The point was he wanted to be himself. He said he would be happier being a car salesman than pretending to be James Bond all his life.

I take away from this the importance of being oneself rather than trying to copy someone else. In a world of today with so many 'models', this is a wise reminder that 'to thy own self be true' as Shakespeare once said.

To return to the idea of selfhood: identifying the 'selfhood' of the child allows me too to believe in a life after death (although I accept that some do not believe this). This means that the human being survives the death experience, although in a different mode. However, while still on planet Earth, the human being is a mysterious unity of elements. Thus when I say 'I', it means me in my totality, my Earthy mode of existence.

Unfortunately, Christianity has too often separated out 'body' and 'soul' as if it was talking about two people. I have found myself increasing cranky with a dualism that separated out our material self with our spiritual self. It often suggest that, as in some kinds of Gnosticism, the material aspect is bad and the spirit good. This is far removed from the Jewish attitude of seeing the human person as a totality of material and spiritual, and living life to the full by enjoying all aspects of life.

Sexuality: changes in attitudes

If I have changed my thinking on human beings, so too with sexuality which is another topic that always evokes interest and strong opinions. What gender, sexuality and sexual orientation are, has been challenged from many philosophical and moral viewpoints, but not least from people's personal experience. It is difficult to gainsay personal experience. The vocabulary around these discussions has increased greatly in my life, with terms like sexual orientation, non-binary, bisexual, trans, transphobic, birthing mother, and gender fluidity and pride. Some of these concepts are completely new to me.

Over my adult years, society in the west, especially in recent centuries, has moved from a very private, prudist Victorian attitude towards sex, to the sexual revolution of the 1960s, to acceptance of homosexuality, lesbianism, bisexual people, trans-gender people, to same sex marriages, childless marriages, freedom of sexual expression, and both implicit and explicit sexual scenes in movies and on telly.

Reproductive technology has made *in vitro fertilisation* possible, as well as artificial insemination and donor babies, and 'wombs for hire'. All these developments add to the complexities of modern life on many levels, not least the ethical level.

I will come back to the topic of sexuality below when I discuss the shocking and horrendous episode of sexual abuse in the Catholic Church.

Marriage

I never gave much thought of marriage other than what I took for granted at home. That was a loving family with one father and one mother, and brothers and sisters. Other families that I knew were much the same in the 1950s. Divorce was frowned upon and seldom mentioned. I took for granted that families were constituted by one father, one mother and the children.

Years later in Rome, in the later 1960s, I experienced something new. A gay Polish man wanted to get out of Poland permanently. He happened to be working in Rome in an international organisation on a limited visa. However, he managed to devise a plan with a consenting Italian woman with whom he was not in love. They would officially get married so that he could then apply for Italian citizenship and escape his homeland. After some time, he could quietly divorce her and he would be free; and so would she. This was new to me: I had never thought of marriage as something to be manipulated like this.

Earlier in my life, going back to the 1960s when I began to think more deeply on some basic issues, my first concern was the value of marriage expressed in the terminology of the so-called 'primary' and 'secondary' aims of marriage. (At the extreme of this mindset was the reductionist statement, cited by Geoffrey Robinson, of one bishop at Vatican II who stated that the principal task of the laity was 'to beget children because of the shortage of vocations to the priesthood'!)[24]

In the past, I thought that saying that the primary aim of marriage was to have children was too narrow and I welcomed the rejection of the categories of 'primary' and 'secondary' with regard to aims. I am happy with a revision of aims and acknowledge the new approach which speaks of aims in general. This includes aspects such as mutual support and seeing sexual intercourse as an expression of love, and marriage as giving support in life to one's partner.

This viewpoint was a breakthrough although it has not percolated down to all the laity perhaps due to the conservative popes that followed Vatican II. (The negative approach to sexual intercourse was also reflected in the preference to see the Canticle of Canticles as metaphorical, rather than literal, in meaning!)

The teachings of Vatican II on the topic were positive I thought, but the rejection of contraception by Paul VI in 1968 (*Humanae Vitae*) was disappointing and not in keeping with the new approach.

With the sexual revolution of the 1960s came the further uncoupling of sexual expression from the context of love for another person. The development of the birth control pill gave women the freedom to access easy and reliable contraception. They were no longer compelled to have more and more children. From seeing the aim of sexual copulation being the production of children, it has become accepted as a normal part of life to be enjoyed and not to be repressed by love, family, religion or state.

Homosexuality and the Catholic Church

I also began to think that the way gay people were treated was wrong.

For me, what is interesting and striking is the ever-increasing gulf between the modern deepening understanding of sexuality and the official line of the Catholic Church. The rules and regulations regarding sexual behaviour of the official teaching do not make sense in the context of the modern insightful and scientific understanding of sexuality. I agree with Geoffrey Robinson, the Sydney Catholic bishop who dared to think for himself, when he says that the teaching on heterosexual love must change before we can better understand homosexuality.[25]

I can recall my understanding of sexuality as I grew up. We were brought up to think a number of things. First, that everyone was heterosexual, everyone (male or female) would be attracted to the opposite sex. Anyone who was homosexual or lesbian was pretending to be that. They were perverts. They were going against that with which they were born.

Secondly, the idea that sexual orientation was one hundred percent solid. It rejected any idea of sexuality being located on a continuum from being firmly heterosexual to being firmly homosexual. This attitude meant that there was no understanding or empathy for anyone who might be between hetero- and homosexuality on the continuum, unsure of their sexual orientation.

Thirdly, a consequence of the above was that one's sexual orientation could not change over the span of one's life. The old idea was that sexual orientation was binary, that is, fixed as either hetero- or homo-sexual.

Medical science has taught us that not everyone is heterosexual. Homosexuals are not 'perverts' but 'inverts', in the sense that they might have a male body but be attracted to the same sex. They are true to the way they feel. Hence the error in thinking that a homosexual's sexual orientation can be changed by medical treatment. We have also learnt that sexual orientation is on a continuum and that it can change over time, over a lifespan for example.

I recall one postgraduate discussion on the topic in which I as involved. I was trying to point out the fact that some people have male (or female) reproductive organs but feel attracted to the same sex. Traditionally, these people were called 'perverts' as we saw above, as if they have perverted their instincts. Impressive though I thought my point was, not all agreed. One male, mature-aged student, after all my arguments drawing on modern insights from psychology and human experience, blithely retorted: 'Well, whatever you say, but if I find a homosexual, I will turn the hose on him'.

Conversion therapy

I recall clearly while studying in Rome in the 1960/70s the way the German Redemptorist moral theologian, Bernard Häring (1912-1998) taught that conversion therapy should be rejected. He came under much scrutiny from the Vatican heresy hunters of his time but he held to his insights which were influenced by researchers into the nature of sexuality.

Häring was not the only Catholic theologian who thought differently to the official line. Way back in 1977, a group of American Catholic moral theologians took a step forward. They were Anthony Kosnik, William Carroll,

Agnes Cunningham, Ronald Modras and James Schulte. They published *Human Sexuality: New Directions in American Catholic Thought*.

I could identify with their position: they found the norms of the Catholic Church too rigid and oppressive. The norms placed too much stress on individual acts instead of on overall intentions relating to growth and integration. This was a new way at looking at the ethical dimensions of acts. At the time, and not surprisingly, the Congregation for the Doctrine of Faith (CDF) rejected their approach.

This left people like me caught between the official line and reformers. We had to teach the official line but would also add that, after all considerations were taken, each individual must follow her/his own conscience. This was, in fact, a teaching of Vatican II which some bishops did not accept. They did not want people to think for themselves. But, of course, many Catholics did, as with the teaching on contraception. I felt the new ideas were worth exploring, not only relating to sexuality but also to complex issues like abortion and euthanasia. Today, there is some progress with Pope Francis asking church leaders to be more open to modern sciences, including sociology and anthropology. I hope this approach continues.

There are signs that it will. I am thinking of the new cardinal of Luxembourg, Jean-Claude Hollerich S.J. who, since March 2022, has been the president of the Commission of the Bishops' Conference of European Union. He has stated quite boldly that the Catholic Church must revisit its teachings on homosexuality. This raised the hackles of a person like the Australian Cardinal, George Pell, who was noted for his strident condemnation of homosexuality.

Hollerich, a Belgian, has studied and worked in Japan. I believe that living and working in a culture other than one's own often leads to a broadening of one's own thinking. Often what helps is engagement with people at the level of their daily lives. This gives an added dimension to one's reflections on life and empathy for individuals. This was certainly my experience of living and working in Italy.

Pope John XXIII worked in Turkey and Eastern Europe, Pope Francis worked in Argentina as well as studying in Europe. There are many other examples. Adding even greater weight to the arguments of these thinkers are those bishops who themselves were sexually abused and now advocate for change. I am thinking of Geoffrey Robinson for example, mentioned above.

I feel that with a new brand of leaders like Hollerich and many others, my church is on a more just and positive pathway. The turning point might well have been *Humanae Vitae* (1968) of Paul VI when many Catholics rejected his teaching on contraceptives. Since then, more and more theologians and ordinary folk have sensed that the Catholic Church needed to update. Sadly, many too have walked away because change has not been forthcoming.

My church, the Catholic Church, painted itself into a corner by adopting a position of refusing to say it was wrong on any point. It has refused to admit making any mistakes, like not condemning slavery and capital punishment. This attitude had made change too difficult. Fortunately, Pope Francis has been able to admit when he (or the church more broadly) has made a mistake and has apologised.

On the point of never being wrong, let me add something that irritates me about the Curia of the Catholic Church. Not only do they not want to say they were wrong on an issue, but in matters of doctrine they insist that there is only one way to express doctrine and that is with their own words. Anyone who knows how difficult it is to express ideas about the transcendent will admit there are different ways in expressing it. An example of this was the series of conversations between Anglicans and Roman Catholics, called ARCIC (Anglican Roman Catholic International Commission). In particular, the statement on the Eucharist which I thought was excellent.

The Roman authorities, after many months of cogitation, responded by saying that they preferred their own way of speaking of the eucharist! This sort of mindset persist in many Catholics today who just cannot see that the language used is not the only possibility, and indeed might be out of date. 'Transubstantiation' has blocked many Catholics from thinking further on the meaning of Eucharist. This still comes up with parishioners I know.

I have also felt the weight of misogyny in the Catholic Church. I have never thought that the issue of women's ordination is a matter of doctrine. I recall at an Australian Catholic Theological Association (ACTA) conference at Manly Seminary, Sydney, in 1984 when Dennis Edwards, the well-known Australian theologian, said he believed that the teaching on male-only ordination was a matter of doctrine. I admired much of his writing but on this matter I disagreed. I have always felt it was just custom (a question of 'discipline') and could be changed overnight by the authorities.

However, I feel different cultures (within a church) should decide what is best for them. Many western cultures can easily accept women pastors, but other cultures might not feel ready for it yet. In the west, I agree with the cardinal who some years ago at an ESCT (European Society of Catholic Theologians) conference in Graz, Austria, which I attended, said the trajectory of women in the church is only going one way – up. The ordination of women will come.

Omega Point

Now let me move the conversation to the end of our journey, to the topic of death – an issue we all have to contemplate. My thinking on death has also changed over the years as one would expect.

During the 2019-2022 Covid-19 virus pandemic, we learnt a lot of things. Not least was some of the Greek alphabet! We had the Alpha strain and then the Delta variant followed by Omicron. Our fear was that we might be asked to go right through the alphabet to Omega, that being the last letter of the 24-letter Greek alphabet.

In classical literature, God is often spoken of as the 'Alpha and Omega', 'The Beginning and the End'. The French palaeontologist, theologian, philosopher and teacher, Pierre Teilhard de Chardin (1881-1955) spoke of the universe as engaged in Christogenesis, becoming more Christ-like, which would be fully realised when it reaches 'Omega Point', at the end of time. Sooner or later, we all have to die to move on in our journey, to return to the Father. And the world, the universe, we believe, will come to an end.

A viral pandemic certainly focuses the mind on death and the future. Death is not a topic that attracts people. Death denial is common. We usually dislike facing our own mortality. Perhaps it is a significant sign of maturity when we finally can confront it.

During the pandemic, the elderly in nursing homes were at particular risk of dying if they could not be vaccinated. Many families saw their loved-ones neglected and dying without anyone even being present. The number of people at funerals was limited, thus isolating grieving families further. Death was all around us, not unlike the *The Black Death* of the fourteenth century which caused the death of between 75 and 200 million people.

During this current era of the pandemic, an incident arose quite unexpectedly. I was on the beach one day with two of my young grandchildren. They were 8 and 5 years old at the time of this incident. We were plodding our way on the beach in our bare feet in a carefree manner enjoying the crisp sea air, when the older of the two asked me, quite out of the blue: 'Oupa (Grandpa), what is heaven like?' I have no idea where this question came from. We had certainly not been talking about religion, God, souls or anything remotely connected with death. In fact the previous topic had been about which ice cream flavours were our favourites.

My reply was that heaven was like a party. Imagine a party with all your friends. Imagine all the likely food and drinks available and the music playing in the background and people dancing. This is what heaven is like if I must express it in a language that an 8-year old will understand.

The image I was thinking of was the feast, banquet, mentioned in the gospel. Heaven is like a feast to which we are invited. The story of the wedding feast occurs in both Matthew's and Luke's Gospel. The king invites us to a wedding feast or banquet where there is food, music, dancing and wine. Everyone – be they young or old – likes a party or feast. This is an universal phenomenon and is chosen as an image of what God has in stall for those who love him. John's Gospel which is very symbolic, starts with a wedding feast which is a symbol of the kingdom, and if you are one hundred percent in the kingdom you are in heaven.

(By the way there is another example of an *image of heaven* which is worth noting. Luke, in his Gospel of Sunday 30 in Ordinary time, year C, says Jesus commented to the good thief, 'Today, you will be with me in paradise'. Not 'heaven' or 'wedding feast', but 'paradise'. This could be read as a reference to Genesis and the Garden of Eden.

And what are the characteristics of that life in Eden? An easy and frequent conversation between God and Adam, relaxed surroundings, peace, abundance of what is needed for life, like food and loving companionship. All that makes up another image of 'heaven'. I have noted that some Egyptian burial chambers at Luxor have depictions of heaven as a place of sunshine and trees loaded with wholesome fruit.)

Or, on a more mystical level, with Richard Rohr and addressing adults, one could say heaven is faith, hope and love to the fullest degree (which is God). They are the only things that last. They are the elements of the Garden of Eden story.

The Catholic Church has many detractors at this point in our history, the twenty-second century – and for some very compelling reasons. But on the positive side, I have always appreciated its funeral liturgies which are a great support to those who grieve. Ideally the community comes together to grieve and participate in the ritual. There is a strong focus on the deceased, their coffin up in the front near the altar, the eulogies, the pictures, the readings and prayers read out aloud by family members or close friends.

One of the key thoughts is the prayer that reminds us that with death, 'life is *changed*, not taken away'. This is key. This is the belief of Christians. One's mode of existence is changed not annihilated. For those who believe, this is a tremendous support as are all the references to 'resurrection' in the liturgy (even though many, I fear, think of *'resuscitation'* when they hear the word *'resurrection'*).

A more helpful way of looking at 'resurrection' which gets away from the idea of the body rising out of the grave, is to see resurrection as the self-emptying and the infilling of Christ. When this process is complete, we are resurrected, the 'omega' point.)

In other cultures, death is dealt with in various ways. I have always been struck by the Australian First Nations people, the Aborigines, who see a very thin veil between this life and the life of the spirits (different modes of existence). Let me give some examples. When Aborigines saw the first British settlers arriving in 1788 they thought they were the ghosts of their forefathers, because they were so white!

In their culture, a woman could conceive a child when passing a billabong of importance because the spirit of the child could leap into her womb as the woman walked past. A raven that lands on your shoulder might be there to tell you that a family member has died. The veil between the two worlds is thin.

In 2002, I went to Darwin and Broome on study leave and, at the suggestion of a friend, I took the plane from Darwin to the Tiwi Islands. It is only twenty minutes by small plane, as I remember. One has hardly climbed into the sky when the plane starts its descent. I landed on Bathurst Island and, on arrival, someone thought I was from the

Health Department in Darwin. I must have looked like a health worker!

In fact, I made my way to the presbytery where I lodged with the parish pastor for a few days and was able to speak to a few elders among the Aborigines. I was also able to see the most impressive church painted with Aboriginal colours and symbols, a sign of how important the inculturation of Christianity in the local culture is. I could go on about the lack of inculturation, but I will restrain myself.

There is plenty of history here. Outside the church nearby, I noted the memorial to Fr John McGrath who warned Darwin (in vain, as it turned out) of the approaching (Japanese) bombers in 1942. Not far away was the museum which commemorates Bishop Xavier Gsell, 'the bishop with 150 wives'. But that is another story.

A strange thing happened to me there on Bathurst Island. Was it coincidence or spooky? It revolved around the name 'Gideon'. A man had just died with that name so they could not use it in public. As it is also my name, the situation was awkward. When introducing me, the pastor had to circumlocute: 'This is my friend – he has the same name as the elder just deceased'.' This custom is part of the burial ritual known as 'Pukumani'.

The Pukumani ceremony is considered the most important ceremony in a person's life: it ensures that the spirit of the dead person goes from the living world into the spirit world, from one mode of existence to another.

The Pukumani, which takes place months after the deceased has been buried, allows Tiwi full expression of their grief and provides a forum for artistic expression through song, dance, sculpture and body painting. (Unlike modernists who wish to deny death.) It was during this stage of 'Gideon's' death that I happened to visit Bathurst Island.

The ceremony brings some kind of closure to the deceased person's life and death on Earth. For the Kiwi people, the final Pukumani is the climax of a series of ceremonies that traditionally continue for many months after the burial of the dead.

There are usually two funeral ceremonies I am told. One at the time of death and a second many months later. A feature of these ceremonies are the *tutini* poles.

The *tutini*, carved from Kartukini or Ironwood, take many months to prepare. They are decorated to celebrate the dead person's life, which is seen as a material and spiritual journey.[26]

All this reinforces for me the importance of ceremony, of burial rites, of the need to acclaim and celebrate the life of the deceased on Earth, not to ignore it as is often done in Western society. Death is part of life, not to be ignored.

Another experience of death happened recently, although in very different cultural circumstances. I attended the funeral of a close friend who had died of cancer. She could have had an operation but chose not to, and moved forward knowing that her time was up. She was very composed and had obviously accepted her forthcoming death with tranquillity.

Tutini on Bathurst Island.

The painted sanctuary in the Catholic Church on Bathurst Island.

Underpinning this was her deep spirituality. For many years, she had been a member of the Christian Life Community (CLC) which is a group of ordinary people leading a life inspired by the (Spiritual) Exercises of St

Ignatius of Loyola. She was always happy (in spite of many tribulations) and loved to dance.

In planning her funeral service, she asked everyone to dress in bright colours and that, together with her choice of joyous hymns, made her farewell a vibrant, happy occasion, which it should be if we see death as a resurrection, as a new mode of existence. I have never experienced a funeral like that. It seems outrageous to say that I (and others) enjoyed the funeral service, but I did. And I am sure she would be happy to know that. Another friend who was told by his oncologist that he only had months to live, wrote with the same deep faith and acceptance of my friend above: 'Perhaps a prayer of thanks would be in order for knowing ahead of time when many people do not. Daily prayer in this condition profits from tighter focus; "Thy will be done" can be said with deeper commitment'.[27]

Some people think that reflection on death is some kind of morbid exercise which should be avoided as negative and anti-life. I would disagree. The Australian actor, Claudia Karvan, says her thinking on death changed after reading *The Tibetan Book of the Living and the Dying*, by Sogyal Rinpoche.[28] She is now more grateful for life itself, is determined not to waste precious time, and reflects on how precious the people who surround her are.

I also think of life as a great privilege and opportunity to do some good on this Earth, however small or insignificant, and then, when temporal life is over, of returning to the embrace of our common Father, or being totally swept up into Spirit's love, in a new way of living.

Bringing it together

Looking back over the last eighty years and my own reflections, much has changed. And one of the changes is that the rate of change has accelerated. I am talking of the western world of developed and developing countries. The grand old fundamentalist view which was taken from the biblical book of Genesis prevailed. Human beings were created at a certain time and then spread and populated the world. The entire world was found around the Mediterranean sea. No one knew what was beyond that world until the voyages of discovery in the fifteenth and sixteenth century. Then, when the New World was discovered, it was thought that the beings that inhabited these regions were savages, or only half human, if at all.

Slowly, as the centuries passed, this view was modified, and by the beginning of the twentieth century, the stereotypes of the nineteenth century anthropology were being challenged. As I grew up, anthropology grew and became more nuanced and progressive. Skin colour was not a determinant in human dignity, people with white skin did not enjoy a higher I.Q. than others. In fact I.Q. was seen as a biased tool.

Progress was made in other areas of study, especially science. My father had no electricity in his home when he was a boy at school. He would use a candle when studying at night. As a boy he saw the first motor car struggling down the main street. My father never travelled by plane as they were new and expensive. I first flew in a plane aged about twenty-one.

About the 1960s, the education world seemed to have realised that teaching science at school required science laboratories, so money was poured into that as the scientific understanding of the world grew in importance. In religion, the study of sacred books from a more objective and scientific perspective grew, although many rejected this approach outright, conflating faith with empirical knowledge.

The old view, as I am calling it, also thought the resources of this world were infinite. They saw human beings as the supreme masters of the universe and their fate; and technology seem to offer all the answers they needed. In this universe, man was superior to woman. White races superior to black. The spiritual world was less important. Religion was relegated to the superstitious category. Science and money were the gods to be worshipped. Progress and development were catchwords.

Growth was unlimited. You could never exhaust the supply of oil, coal, copper, water, food, or whatever . This was called into question by a group of people called the Club of Rome, as we saw above, founded in 1968 in Rome. It was a non-profit informal organisation of business people and leaders brought together to discuss global issues. In 1972, it produced its first report entitled *The Limits to Growth*. That says it all.

About the same time, the new understanding of the universe known as the New Creation Story became popular. That is the big Bang Theory. This was that the universe started from a singularity and expanded into what we have today with the universe continuing to expand at enormous rates.

The Big Bang was about 13.8m billion years ago. Our planet evolved much later, and we, the human beings, even later than that. We are late arrivals as far as the history of our planet goes.

We have worked out, through archaeological work and anthropology, that people did not develop in a straight line from hunter-gatherers to farmers but there was great diversity and sophistication in the way people lived and developed technologies. I think of the book entitled, *The Weirdest People in the World*,[29] where WEIRD stands for 'western, educated, industrial, rich, democratic'. Currently that debate continues among authors like Pascoe,[30] Peter Sutton and Keryn Walshe.[31]

What difference have all these changes made for me? I have had to adapt like most other people. I now see humans as and Earthlings, as the products of a long process of development. I see the planet as our home which we have not cared for in the past. I see it as most urgent that we change our ways of living, minimise pollution, avoid fossil fuels, look after our waterways and oceans, in order to care for our planet appropriately.

For this to happen, we must identify the common good and reject all the selfish individualism that characterises much of western society.

I have had to question many assumptions that were taken as given in my childhood, such as the inequality of genders, races, nations, and reject the idea that our resources are unlimited.

I have begun to appreciate the wonders of creation in a new way. I think about the beauty of the flora and fauna that surrounds us and have become more aware of other universes and stars and planets and see how small we are in the big scheme of things.

From archaeological findings, I have learnt about ancient tribes and nations from the centuries before the time of Christ, that we never knew existed. I have had cause to re-evaluate their intelligence and technologies.

I have also seen the tendency to see world only in terms of its material dimension. In rejecting the superstitious and extreme in religion, many have rejected the spiritual entirely. I see this as a big mistake. There is a tendency to see science as capable of solving all problems. Modern technologies, with all their pros and cons, will not solve all our problems. In spite of all the negativity in the world, I am optimistic. I believe we have the capacity to correct our ways and find solutions to what threatens us. Without hope, human beings cannot live. My religion points out the centrality of hope, faith and love.

Endnotes

[1] There were five of us: Anton (1934-2021), Margaret b. 1936, Bernard b. 1938, Gideon b. 1941, Jeannette b. 1947.

[2] Robert Travers, *Murder in the Blue Mountains*, Melbourne: Hutchinson Group, 1972.

[3] David Graeber and David Wengrow, The Dawn of Everything: A New History of Humanity , Penguin Books, 2021, p. 38.

[4] https://www.unhcr.org/en-au/figures-at-a-glance.html, referenced on 19.04.2022.

[5] Eddie Jaku, *The Happiest Man on Earth*, Sydney: Macmillan Australia, 2020, 11.

[6] David Graeber and David Wengrow, *The Dawn of Everything: A New History of Humanity*, Penguin Books, 2021, p. 20.

[7] Op.cit., 154.

[8] Op.cit.,, 155.

[9] Op.cit., 175.

[10] Op.cit., 165.

[11] I was a member of the Australian Catholic Theological Association (ACTA), the Catholic Theological Society of America (CTSA) and the European Society for Catholic Theologians (ESCT). Attending these conferences enabled me to gain insights into various theologies and cultures. After the Fall of the Berlin Wall, a big influx of theologians from Eastern Europe gave the ESCT a new dimension.

[12] Cf. John Philip Newell, *The Rebirthing of God*, Nashville: Christian Journeys, 10.

[13] David Marr, *Killing for Country*, Melbourne: Black Inc. 2023.

[14] Diarmuid O'Murchu, *Doing Theology in an Evolutionary Way*, Maryknoll NY: Orbis, 2021.

[15] Linda Jaivin, *The Shortest History of China*, Melbourne: Black Inc., 2021, 33.

[16] Alan Richardson, *The Political Christ*, SCM, Canterbury, 1973

[17] https://www.hindustantimes.com/world-news/pope-francis-thanks-journalists-fo accessed on 5.5.2022.

[18] Gideon Goosen and Margaret Tomlinson, *Studying the Gospels*, Sydney: E. J. Dwyer, 1994.

[19] David Marr, Op.cit., Melbourne: Black Inc. 2023, 256.

[20] https://www.washingtonpost.com/world/2022/10/15/malta-daphne-caruana-galizia-murder/
[21] Geoffrey Robinson, *Towards The End of My Days*, Mulgrave, Vic.: Garratt Publishing, 2020, 372.
[22] John Paul II, *Ut unum sint*, 25 May 1995, #96.
[23] Joseph Henrich, *The Weirdest People in the World*, Penguin, 2019, 21.
[24] Robinson, Op.cit., 377.
[25] Robinson, Op.cit.
[26] https://tiwilandcouncil.com/index.cfm?fuseaction=page&p=249&l=2&id=60&smid=121 accessed 6.7.2012.
[27] Charles Hill, 'Going to God', *Word in Life*, February, 2007. 41-43.
[28] Claudia Karvan, *The Good Weekend*, 18 March 2023, 30
[29] Joseph Henrich, *The Weirdest People on Earth*, Penguin, 2020.
[30] Bruce Pascoe, *Dark Emu*, Broome: Magabala Books, 2014.
[31] Peter Sutton and Keryn Walshe, *Farmers or Hunter-gatherers?*, Melbourne: Melbourne University Press, 2021

www.ingramcontent.com/pod-product-compliance
Lightning Source LLC
Chambersburg PA
CBHW012005090526
44590CB00026B/3879